For Unto Us A Child Is Born

Devotions from the Pastime Preachers

Ted Keen and John Brantley, Editors

Buckeye Creek Press

ISBN : 978-2-345-67890-8

Published by Buckeye Creek Press

Table of Contents

A Story of Introduction

It was cold that winter. The prelude to the December frost actually started in November of that year.

The newspapers started early with little faces of Santa peeking through the pages of the news trying to encourage early shopping.

It was cold that winter. Snow turned into ice and daily you could hear the – footsteps of what appeared to be giants – tracking through the frozen snow.

It was cold that winter, and the bells were being heard throughout the churches. The colors were red, green, gold, purple, and white, just as they will be this year.

The frost on the inside of the window gathered, resulting from the steam heat. The lights flickered from the tree.

"Angels We Have Heard on High" and "Silver Bells" made their way through the static of the AM Radio. It was cold that year.

Clinging cash registers, men wearing long black winter coats, fedoras and galoshes. Women in coats, hats, scarves, gloves and whatever else they could find to stay warm. It was cold that winter.

The blistering storms of that year were in no way a match for "His Coming." I can readily recall "Come Thou Long Expected Jesus", "O Come, O Come, Emmanuel", and there were songs I could not even pronounce. Mr. Wooten, the Choir Master, had practiced the songs to perfection. They'd better sing right. He had a stick in his right hand that seemed to effectively guide the music.

Something big was about to happen. In my small way, I wanted to have a part. It was cold that year.

The human effort to set the stage was simple. Choir rehearsals, shopping for gifts, baking, and kind words of Merry Christmas. O, how I wish those kind, generous, heartfelt words would come back again. Christmas trees, lights, dancing, mannequins in the downtown stores…what a delight!

Christmas cards that filled the mailboxes on a daily basis. We could not wait to open them. An evening ritual of card opening was exciting. We liked the card from Auntie. It always had one dollar apiece for each of us.

Finally, Christmas Eve arrived. Poppa Jack waited until Big Mama went to bed before he would bring out the brandy. According to his mark on the bottle, it hadn't been touched since last year. One bottle every six years was good.

We were all inside that evening. Boxes crowded the tree, seeking a place of importance. They were decorated with a rainbow of bows. The smell of fresh paint gave way to seasonal smells.

The time had come. We now heard the gospel. Daddy read the Christmas Story from the old Bible. The gospel silenced the cares of the world. The cold turned to warm. The noise of time was silenced. The glow of the moment would be centered around His Birth. Santa took a backseat. "For unto us a Child is born."

The printing of this book reflects the thoughts of friends within the Griffin District. It is my prayer that you will be blessed by the scriptures, stories and prayers during this Advent and Christmas Season.

Richard D. Winn
Griffin District Superintendent
North Georgia Conference of the United Methodist Church

December 1

> *The angel of the Lord called to Abraham a second time from heaven, and said, "By myself I have sworn, says the Lord: Because you have done this, and have not withheld your son, I will indeed bless you, and I will make your offspring as numerous as the stars of heaven and as the sand that is on the seashore. And your offspring shall possess the gate of their enemies, and by your offspring shall all the nations of the earth gain blessing for themselves, because you have obeyed my voice."*
> *Genesis 22:15-18*

It is a principle in Scripture that obedience brings blessing. In the passage prior to these verses we see Abraham's obedience in offering his son Isaac as a burnt offering at God's command. Thankfully for Isaac, the angel of the Lord intervened when Abraham was about to bring the knife down! Abraham's intent to obey was enough for God. In our text we see that as a result of Abraham's obedience, blessing was promised to him. But God is gracious and has also promised blessing to his descendants. Not stopping there, God promised blessing to the entire world through Abraham's offspring. What a God!

It is God's nature to be generous, to bring blessing to all who will receive it. Through Abraham's descendants the nations of the world have indeed been blessed. It was to those offspring that God sent the Holy Scriptures. The commandments, the prophets, the psalms, the histories of God's work among His people are all in the Old Testament, given to and through the offspring of Abraham. Throughout these scriptures we see that those who blessed Israel were blessed by the God of heaven. It is in these scriptures that the promise of a Messiah who would come and make all things right was given.

The ultimate fulfilling of this promise to Abraham came about in the arrival of the promised Messiah. Through Him, "all the nations of the earth" are indeed blessed. At this time of year particularly, we are mindful of the coming of that promised one. During Advent we as the followers of Jesus the Messiah, relive to some degree the time of waiting and expectation that Abraham's offspring lived with every day. God's people, the Jews, Abraham's children, lived with the promise of Messiah for generations.

At last, in God's perfect time, He arrived. With His arrival has come blessing for all who receive Him. Peace, hope, forgiveness, love, and Life with a capital L...abundant life, all come to us through the work of Jesus. Remember where all this started? With one man being obedient. With one man who loved God more than his own son. With one man who listened when God spoke. We too can listen. We too can be obedient. We too can share the blessings God gives us. As we do, who knows where the blessing will end?

Ed Swehla
County Line UMC

Prayer: Lord of Life, we pray today that we will hear when you call us. We desire to obey when we understand your direction. We thank you for your generosity, for your abundant blessings in our lives. Grant us opportunity to share your blessings with others as we wait for the appearing again of your promised Son. In the Name of Jesus we pray. Amen.

December 2

> *Then Isaiah said: "Hear then, O house of David!*
> *Is it too little for you to weary mortals, that you weary*
> *my God also? Therefore the Lord himself will give you a*
> *sign. Look, the young woman is with child and shall*
> *bear a son, and shall name him Immanuel. He shall eat*
> *curds and honey by the time he knows how to refuse the*
> *evil and choose the good.*
> *Isaiah 7:13-15*

My wife holds the marketing honor, having convinced the good people at Krispy Kreme Donuts to post a bright red neon sign whenever they have hot fresh donuts on the line. I feel like Pavlov's dogs when the little red light flashes and the tone rings on my smart phone. It reports "hot ones" and how many miles to my nearest location.

Signs like these make it easy to know when and where to find those delicious morsels. Now my cardiologist needs to have an app that comes on to remind me to take my blood pressure whenever the donuts light up my phone.

The role of the prophet is to be a messenger for God's people. They most often read, interpret and share God's signs that the people cannot or will not see. Prophets are the light shining in dark times and through the obvious words of caution and warning, yet the world can stare at the truth and see what it chooses to see.

I had a 'big-brother' moment this week where I received a clear sign that I knew I was being watched. I went into Barnes and Nobel to buy a book and used my credit card to make the purchase. As I was walking out the door I received a text from my card company to try out the restaurant across the street. That sign made me feel uncomfortable.

Sometimes, even though the signs are not easy, we need someone speaking, flashing, texting or jumping-up-and-down to remind us where we are and where we need to be going. Isaiah lived hundreds of years prior to Jesus and yet begins to tell of God's signs in order to get our attention.

One day, I was following the GPS mapping directions on my phone to find a cut through in an area I had not driven through in several years. I was glad to find an easy route. The monotone voice droned with the radio and the other conversations in the car every tenth of a mile as our next turn drew closer and closer.

Despite all the warning when it came time to turn I was in the far left lane to make the right hand turn. So I had to turn off the radio, ask for quiet in the car and let the device reconfigure the best, next directions. We made it to the restaurant to meet our friends, but even with all the help and suggestions, I had to focus on one thing to find my way.

Isaiah's words to Israel remind us to not grow weary, but to see God is working to bring us together. Listen, God is speaking to us. Look for a sign. Look for a young woman with a child named Immanuel. I suppose Isaiah could have developed a network of every mid-wife and ask them to report the mothers that named their children Immanuel.

As it turns out, Mary and Joseph, of whom Isaiah foretells, are far from home and have no one with them when Jesus is born. Couldn't Isaiah have come up with an easier sign to see? And, why did he have to give notice such a long time ahead?

Some folks like to plan ahead and others wait to the last possible moment. When these two conflicting personalities end up in one household through marriage, it is certainly an obstacle that affects everyday life. I invite you to see the opportunity for balance, rather than the conflict of different signs.

We plan ahead so that we have options when the last minute comes. If we were waiting for God to speak through a single husband and wife, having a child while visiting out of town in the dark of the night, we might miss it. But with hundreds of years of anticipation, we have the greater chance of more people being on board with anticipation.

Isaiah is telling us what to watch for in our time of waiting. He also tells us that the time is also limited. The warning is that this child named Immanuel is born to a young mother and will be faced with evil, while still eating baby food.

This is a mixed message about the coming Messiah. God is about to reveal God's self to us through this sign, but no sooner than it happens, evil will try to threaten and cover up the sign.

One of the things I dislike about commercial Christmas is that, before the sun sets on the 25th of December, the decorations begin to come down and the commercial sell-off clears the way for the next holiday. Not only are their twelve days in the season of Christmas, the sign is not about shopping days and gifts. The season is about Isaiah's message from God.

God promises to come to us, self-revealed through a young mother, a weary father and a child named "God-is-with-us." If the decorations and traditions that you celebrate in this month are not leading you to find God with us, then maybe they are not signs you need to be following.

Instead of sharing the traditional greeting, "Merry Christmas," try sharing this one: "May Christ be with us!" Show the world the sign that has been promised for twenty five hundred years. Use all the tools, technologies, conversations and cards to shine the light of Jesus Christ: God is with us still.

John Brantley
Jackson UMC

Prayer: God show us the signs of your Son and may we become signs of Christ for others. Amen.

December 3

> *But you, O Bethlehem of Ephrathah, who are one of the little clans of Judah, from you shall come forth for me one who is to rule in Israel, whose origin is from of old, from ancient days. Therefore he shall give them up until the time when she who is in labor has brought forth; then the rest of his kindred shall return to the people of Israel. And he shall stand and feed his flock in the strength of the LORD, in the majesty of the name of the LORD his God. And they shall live secure, for now he shall be great to the ends of the earth; and he shall be the one of peace.*
> *Micah 5:2-5a*

A few years ago I visited the Holy Land for the first time with a group of clergy and laity. Seeing the storied places of the Bible was a profound spiritual experience for me, deepening my preaching and teaching – and my appreciation for the Bible. I was struck by how some descriptive passages of scripture came to life for me as I sat on a boat in the middle of the Sea of Galilee and traveled through the Judean wilderness, and prayed at the Western Wall in Jerusalem. Yet, the shrines and churches, bazaars and gift shops, cell phones and cameras engulfing most of the holy sites also reminded me how things had changed. It was an odd blending, if not a clash, of old and new, past and present that left me pondering the future.

One of my most vivid experiences was passing through Jerusalem on the way to Bethlehem one day. It was a Saturday, and the city was shut down for the observance of the Sabbath. Our itinerary purposely took us that day to Bethlehem, populated by Christians and Muslims, a city of 25,000 people very much opened for business – especially tourists.

Bethlehem. When we hear or read of it in scripture, we tend to think of a small, humble little town from ancient, biblical days. Scenes of green, quiet pastures, watchful shepherds and of course, an inn, most readily come to mind. But its biblical history goes back much further. Bethlehem is also the place where Jacob buried his wife Rachel nearly 4000 years ago; where Ruth gleaned in the fields and married Boaz; and where their great-grandson David was born and later anointed by Samuel to become the greatest king of Israel.

Micah tells of another king coming who will be born in little Bethlehem, "one who is to rule in Israel, whose origin is from old, from ancient of days" (v2a) and yet one who will be like a shepherd who will "stand and feed his flock." (v.4) King and shepherd he will be, and also "one of peace." (v5a)

These last, descriptive words stir my mind and heart as I think of travelling between Jerusalem and Bethlehem on that Sabbath day. I appreciated seeing the Church of the Nativity, traditionally believed to hold the very place where Jesus was born; and fields where shepherds still pasture their flocks, reminding me of the angel who brought some shepherds tidings of great joy on that holy night long ago.

But what impacted me most was approaching a security check point from Jerusalem to Bethlehem and seeing a thick, 25 foot high concrete wall between Israel and the West Bank. The sight of young, heavily-armed soldiers at the check point, and a wall stretching as far as the eyes can see, separating what is for many the holiest city in the world from surrounding towns was troubling. This wall gives way to a multi-layered wire fence in some areas and it all goes by many names, depending on one's perspective: security fence, separation fence, anti-terrorist fence, racial segregation wall, even Apartheid Wall. For some it's about security and peace. For others it is about segregation and oppression. Some say this constructed barrier is very effective, pointing to the decline in suicide bombings since its construction. Others say it only deepens the resentment that will lead to more determined acts of terrorism, if not war, one way or another. I do not know.

What I do know is that it tells how broken our world truly is. Try as we might, with all our might, we cannot make lasting peace by our own desires and devices. We need God's help. We need the One who can save us from all this, save us from ourselves. We need the One who brings with him the peace of God's kingdom of love and grace. The kind of everlasting peace that the ruler and shepherd from Bethlehem brings, so that all may dwell secure.

Dana Overton-Garrett
Barnesville First UMC

Prayer: Gracious God, the peace of this world is never lasting. We long for the peace that is everlasting, coming to us in the ruler and shepherd born in Bethlehem. Amen.

December 4

> *The people who walked in darkness have seen a great light; those who lived in a land of deep darkness— on them light has shined. You have multiplied the nation, you have increased its joy; they rejoice before you as with joy at the harvest, as people exult when dividing plunder. For the yoke of their burden, and the bar across their shoulders, the rod of their oppressor, you have broken as on the day of Midian. For all the boots of the tramping warriors and all the garments rolled in blood shall be burned as fuel for the fire.*
> *Isaiah 9:2-5*

My family and I experienced the Dialogue in the Dark exhibition when it came to Atlantic Station in Atlanta. During the Dialogue in the Dark experience, lights are turned out in the exhibit and sighted people are led by blind guides through rooms equipped with sound, scent, temperature and wind to simulate the different environments of a park, a city street, a boat at dock and a restaurant.

About a dozen people at a time are given canes and are guided though the exhibit by a blind leader. The leader led us up the dock and into the rocking boat; he led us into the park and encouraged us to feel the grass where the sidewalk ended; he led us along a city street where we could feel the parked car and hear the traffic. The experience is disconcerting to sighted people because, for an hour, we lose control.

We could not navigate by ourselves; we could not steer ourselves away from fire hydrants that knock the shins or the edge of the boat dock where you might lose your footing. We did not know to go left or right to get out.

We got separated from the folks we came with, and some people got unwanted contact from strangers.

Before Jesus came, the world stumbled in the darkness. People could not navigate without the compass that He became for us. They could not steer themselves away from bad decisions; they were often cruel to each other; they did not know their left from their right on many things. They did not know how to get out of this life alive.

But Jesus *did* come. He came and with Him came the knowledge of a God who loves us, an understanding of who we are, an understanding of right and wrong, a Guide who holds our hand, a Way out when there seems to be no way.

Our joy increased just as was predicted in Isaiah: we rejoice just as people do after a harvest. We have the Bread of Life and we will hunger no more. We rejoice as people do when dividing plunder: the battle is over, the victory is won. Jesus defeated sin and death for us and has opened the way for us to share in the divine riches of God! Hallelujah! We once walked in darkness, but now the light of God's love has shined on us, and it changes everything.

Sherri Studdard
Aldora UMC & Ebenezer UMC

Prayer: Father of Light, You came into our darkness and took us by the hand. You have shown us the way to go. You have shown us the way to life abundant and eternal. We thank You for the victory that You have won for us in Jesus. In His precious name we pray. Amen.

December 5

> *For a child has been born for us, a son given to us; authority rests upon his shoulders; and he is named Wonderful Counselor, Mighty God, Everlasting Father, Prince of Peace. His authority shall grow continually, and there shall be endless peace for the throne of David and his kingdom. He will establish and uphold it with justice and with righteousness from this time onwards and for evermore. The zeal of the LORD of hosts will do this.*
> *Isaiah 9:6-7*

As I learn more about being a father to my wonderful four year, I remember that the dark can be a scary place. When my daughter was three years old she required complete darkness to go sleep, and now at the age of four she has to have a night light on to sleep. If the power goes out, her mommy or I will go into the room and sleep with her just in case she happens to wake up and the lights are out. I am now remembering how scary the darkness can be.

When I was a child, my brother and I would go visit our grandparents. While we loved to go to their house, they had one room that was scarier than all the rest: the basement. Basements can be scary. There were times my grandmother would ask my brother and me to retrieve something from the basement or put something down there.

We would turn on a light that would emit a soft glow, run down the steps, do the business we were told to do, and get out of there just as quick. If it were not for the soft glow of a light bulb, I would not have ever gone down into that cold, dark, damp filled room. The dark was an intimidating thing. When the lights went out, my mind would instantly start to see those shadows move. My imagination could convince me that there were in fact monsters in the corners and evil creatures in the laundry area that made horrific noises. (Now I know it was the sump pump.)

Light bulbs and nightlights are incredible little devices. That little bit of light in a dark place can be the difference between a solid night's sleep and hours of fear for a child. That little bit of light can be the difference between a stubbed toe and making it safely to the bathroom for an adult in the middle of the night. When it gets dark, a little bit of light is a good thing.

When we watch the news or read the newspaper or just live in the world, we can tell that it can get pretty dark at times, and I'm not just speaking of a moonless night. A light sucking cancer has infiltrated every aspect of this world. A life draining disease has limited the earth's inhabitants. Our own desires have turned us into a nation of people bumbling and fumbling around in the dark. The evil and wickedness we see in the world is downright suffocating. The filth and nastiness we sometimes see in ourselves is downright terrifying.

However, Christmas is all about lights; lights on the home, lights on the tree and, most importantly by far, a light in a manger in Bethlehem. This light can multiply a nation. It can bring joy to those who only know sorrow and despair. It can break the bondage of oppression. It can bring peace to each of us and to the world around us. Join me in praising the light of the world this Christmas: the light of the world who came to free us from our sins. A light has dawned. His name is Jesus. He came to forgive us of our sins.

Terry Hunter
Williamson UMC

Prayer: Heavenly Father we praise and thank you for sending Jesus to live as a perfect example and for coming to die for our sins. Send your Spirit to us to strengthen our faith in the Light of the World. Work through us to bring the light of Christ to this dark world that so desperately needs him. In Jesus' name we pray. Amen.

December 6

> *A shoot shall come out from the stump of Jesse, and a branch shall grow out of his roots. The spirit of the LORD shall rest on him, the spirit of wisdom and understanding, the spirit of counsel and might, the spirit of knowledge and the fear of the LORD. His delight shall be in the fear of the LORD. He shall not judge by what his eyes see, or decide by what his ears hear; but with righteousness he shall judge the poor, and decide with equity for the meek of the earth; he shall strike the earth with the rod of his mouth, and with the breath of his lips he shall kill the wicked. Righteousness shall be the belt around his waist, and faithfulness the belt around his loins.*
> *Isaiah 11:1-5*

A stump represents the end of the life of a tree. When a tree has reached the end of its life, we cut it down.

At our homeplace, we have an apple tree that has provided fruit for four generations. When my parents first bought the home, it had the apple tree, a pear tree, several plum and peach trees. It felt like the garden of Eden, walking out into the yard and eating the fruit directly from the trees.

Now, the plum trees and peach trees are all dead. They have been cut down. The apple tree which has provided fruit for our family is nearing the end of its life. I remember the wonderful apple pies that my mother would bake from this tree's fruit. I have pruned the tree to keep it alive, but I have not yet brought myself to cut it down. I know that when I cut it down, like the other trees, its life and ability to provide for our family will end. I have not yet lost hope that I can save the tree. This passage tells us that when we have lost all hope, God brings life. "A shoot will come up from the stump of Jesse."

God's people were struggling with their faith. They believed that God would restore the kingdom of Israel, but it looked dead and hopeless. The Romans had taken over the known world and Israel was a captive state. Some of the Roman rulers were ruthless in establishing their control over the region. The Israelites were struggling with their faith in God restoring the kingdom of David.

In the north end of Monroe County are many stumps left from a tornado which tore through the county. It was the largest and widest tornado this area had ever seen. It destroyed scores of homes. It wiped out beautiful mature forests. Through all of this devastation, God has brought life and strength. Many of the neighbors reached out to help one another. Friendships were born. Homes were rebuilt. In the midst of the tragedy, it can tend to look hopeless. God brings restoration and redemption in times when it appears that Satan has won. God brings triumph through tragedy.

In my life, there were a few times that I *felt* were hopeless. They were times when it appeared that all was lost. I remember the hopelessness that I felt when my high school sweetheart and I broke up. I remember the anguish of losing my mother one memory at a time to Alzheimer's disease. I remember losing my life savings which were invested in Real Estate during the great recession. Every time, God brought good from the tragedy. I admit, in the middle of the pain, I wrestled with God. Somehow, when I realized that He had won, I won also. He conquered my doubts. He conquered my fears. He conquered my selfish pride. All of the things that would have destroyed me if left unchecked, He conquered and thereby restored my life.

This world is lost and without hope. God sent His Son to restore righteousness, faith, hope, and love.

Through Jesus, we have our relationship with God restored, we have our true identity and personhood restored. Through Jesus we are delivered from the penalty and power of sin. Through Jesus, we experience true life as God intended it.

Just like the shoot coming from the stump, it is truly in dying to self that we become truly alive. Jesus goes below the surface of our lives and deals with the core of our being, our heart, our spirit.

Keith Harris
Christ UMC

Prayer: Father, thank you for your Son. Thank you for loving us, redeeming us and restoring us. Help us to appropriate into our lives all that Jesus provided through His death and resurrection. Give us hope in the midst of tragedy. Give us faith to trust you when things aren't going as we think they should. Give us love, that we may live as you design. Amen.

> *The wolf shall live with the lamb, the leopard*
> *shall lie down with the kid, the calf and the lion and the*
> *fatling together, and a little child shall lead them. The*
> *cow and the bear shall graze, their young shall lie down*
> *together; and the lion shall eat straw like the ox. The*
> *nursing child shall play over the whole of the asp, and*
> *the weaned child shall put its hand on the adder's den.*
> *They will not hurt or destroy on all my holy mountain;*
> *for the earth will be full of the knowledge of the Lord as*
> *the waters cover the sea.*
> *Isaiah 11:6-9*

Isaiah 11 proclaims the coming of the Messiah, the anointed one of Israel, who will judge with righteousness and equity and will strike down the wicked. These were comforting words for a people who had witnessed destruction at the hands of the Assyrians seven centuries before Christ.

As these four verses reveal, the purpose of the coming Messiah was not revenge against enemies, but a peaceful and just kingdom. This is a beautiful message for us to hear today.

In a world of government shutdowns, corporate shenanigans and ever-present violence, we seem to believe that life is a "zero-sum game," where everyone is out for themselves and only the victorious will survive. This is not the vision from God we find in Isaiah. Rather, we are told that predator and prey will live together, eat together and play together. What a striking contrast to our values!

The coming Messiah doesn't simply judge people, but his leadership will inaugurate a new order to creation.

Seemingly natural enemies not only live side-by-side, but also thrive in the presence of each other. They raise their children together, a vision of families coming together to lift everyone up. We even discover that this coming peace ensures that the weakest and youngest children will be kept safe in the most dangerous circumstances. We find ourselves imagining a world that can be, rather than settling for the world as it already is. That is the message of Christmas.

As a church pastor, people occasionally approach me to ask about how they can help others during this season. Do you know of a group that donates toys and clothes to children? Is there a family nearby that may need food for Christmas supper? Will you let me know if an elderly person needs a lift to the store? At no other time of the year is there such a powerful desire be Christian.

I have a preacher friend who doesn't care for the Christmas season too much. He believes that it is overly commercialized, concentrating too much on Santa, gifts and decorations, almost to the extent that Jesus is forgotten. He much prefers Easter, when the whole world seems to know what is important.

Yet, I have always seen Christmas as an opportunity. With everyone watching, churches and Christians get to shine.

As followers of the one who was born so humbly in Bethlehem, we can participate with God in the recreation and transformation of the world. To paraphrase Francis of Assisi, we can preach the gospel everywhere and use words only when necessary. People are watching and listening. We can lead our lives in December as if nothing special is happening. We can bicker and complain that stores say "Happy Holidays" instead of "Merry Christmas." We can wear ourselves out wrapping, baking and decorating. Or, we can roll up our sleeves and get to work, making a small ripple in our little corner of the world, with the expectation that God will make giant ripples throughout the world.

Nothing is impossible with God! "The earth will be full of the knowledge of the Lord as the waters cover the sea." Wolves and lambs. Leopards and goats. Lions and calves. And there, lying in a manger surrounded by a village too crowded to house him, is the little child who will lead them all.

Ted Keen
Ebenezer UMC

Prayer: O God, don't let us crowd out Jesus in the busyness of this season. Send your Holy Spirit to fill our hearts with your will. May we be instruments of your peace in a world full of predators and prey. Amen.

December 8

> *Sing to the LORD a new song! Sing to the LORD, all the earth! Sing to the LORD! Bless his name! Share the news of his saving work every single day! Declare God's glory among the nations; declare his wondrous works among all people.*
> *Psalm 96:1-3*

Ms. Gilbert was our choir leader. She had a voice that could calm a baby and fill the sanctuary with God's love. She taught me how to sing the hymns of our church. My most favorite time of the year was Christmas. As we prepared for the midnight service on Christmas Eve, my heart was filled with love for God. And then that wonder-filled night came. The church was decorated with poinsettias and holly and filled with people. The Nativity was placed on the altar and the baby Jesus was being prepared to be brought in and placed in the manger at the right moment. And then the organ would begin to be played and it was as if the world stopped just for that holy moment as we heard the story of our Lord's birth. What a special time.

What is it about singing Christmas songs that fills our hearts and spirits with joy? We can't wait for Advent to come and go before we begin singing those Christmas songs. All the churches I've served want to begin singing Christmas before it's time. Of course each year the radio stations and television begin playing those Christmas songs a little earlier. And while some folks complain, all have to admit these songs put a little "pep" in your step. They bring us to remembering Christmas in the past. They bring us to remember the special times in church and at home with family. But for some, they remind us of heartache and pain as we remember a loved one who is no longer with us or a painful memory from childhood.

The Psalmist in Psalm 96 reminds us to sing! Sing in the good times and sing in the not so good times because in all times God is faithful! We are to share God's faithfulness with others.

Psalm 96 speaks of the "fairness" of GOD in an unjust and unfair world. We are to "Sing to The Lord" with gratitude because GOD is our strength and our refuge. Our GOD is our Creator, Sustainer, Father, Savior and Guide. Surely during this season of Advent while we are waiting for the Babe born in a manger, we can find the love and grace in our lives. The world isn't our home, it is a stepping stone to the glory of GOD through the one who has come and who is coming again to bring us to our heavenly home. When we open our eyes to The Lord, we will be filled with love and grace and joy! Let this day be a day of singing the praises of our God.

Liza Marler
Mt. Zion UMC

Prayer: Heavenly God, thank you for today. Thank you for the grace, joy and love of this day. Help us to sing with joy your praises. Help us to be reminded of your amazing grace through the birth of our Lord, Jesus. May our lives be joy-filled as we sing and share your love to others. In Jesus' name. Amen.

December 9

> *Kings of the earth and all peoples, princes and all rulers of the earth! Young men and women alike, old and young together! Let them praise the name of the LORD, for his name alone is exalted; his glory is above earth and heaven. He has raised up a horn for his people, praise for all his faithful, for the people of Israel who are close to him. Praise the LORD!*
> *Psalm 148:11-14*

The one hundred forty-eighth Psalm is a vision of praise. The movements in these verses are of praise from heaven, earth and all human kind. All worship the creator, all praise the Lord. The pattern is like that of an orchestra warming up. When the conductor lifts the baton the sounds of discord become sounds of beautiful music.

Praise does not always come natural. We do not always feel like praising God. Saint Paul taught that we are to rejoice in the Lord always (in all circumstances), again I say rejoice. When we continue to praise Him in spite of our feelings, our attitudes change for the better.

Let me share a story about John Wesley I read some time ago from *Our Daily Bread*:

John Wesley was 21 years of age when he went to Oxford University. He came from a Christian home, and he was gifted with a keen mind and good looks. Yet in those days he was a bit snobbish and sarcastic.

One night, however, something happened that set in motion a change in Wesley's heart. While speaking with a porter, he discovered that the poor fellow had only one coat and lived in such impoverished conditions that he didn't even have a bed. Yet he was an unusually happy person, filled with gratitude to God.

Wesley, being immature, thoughtlessly joked about the man's misfortunes. "And what else do you thank God for?" he said with a touch of sarcasm. The porter smiled and, in the spirit of meekness, replied with joy, "I thank Him that He has given me my life and being, a heart to love Him, and above all a constant desire to serve Him!" Deeply moved, Wesley recognized that this man knew the meaning of true thankfulness.

Many years later, in 1791, John Wesley lay on his deathbed at the age of 88. Those who gathered around him realized how well he had learned the lesson of praising God in every circumstance. Despite Wesley's extreme weakness, he began singing the hymn, "I'll **praise** My Maker While I've Breath."

That hymn was written by Isaac Watts in 1719. Here are the words:

I'll praise my Maker while I've breath;
And when my voice is lost in death,
Praise shall employ my nobler powers
May days of praise shall ne'er be past
While life, and thought, and being last
Or immortality endures.

Happy are they whose hopes rely
on Israel's God who made the sky
and earth and seas, with all their train;
whose truth for ever stands secure,
who saves th'oppressed and feeds the poor,
for none shall find God's promise vain

The Lord pours eyesight on the blind;

The Lord supports the fainting mind
and sends the laboring conscience peace
God helps the stranger in distress,
The widow and the fatherless,
And grants the prisoner sweet release.

I'll praise my God who lends me breath;
and when my voice is lost in death,
Praise shall employ my nobler powers.
My days of praise shall ne'er be past,
While life, and thought, and being last,
or immortality endures.

As we move toward the Christmas season, sometimes we will find ourselves stressed up and stressed out. For some, Christmas is the hardest time of the year to face. The sale of alcohol, aspirin, and anti-depressants will be at an all-time high.

Scripture teaches us to praise the Lord. From the heavens and earth to all of mankind and all of creation. Praise the Lord. Let's keep praising the Lord or some may say keep singing.

Some may wonder what to sing. I've always found that the Doxology helps me.

Ken Stephens
Forsyth UMC

Prayer: Praise God from whom all blessings flow; praise Him, all creatures here below; praise Him above, ye heavenly host; praise Father, Son and Holy Ghost. Amen.

December 10

> *O Lord, our Sovereign, how majestic is your name in all the earth! You have set your glory above the heavens. Out of the mouths of babes and infants you have founded a bulwark because of your foes, to silence the enemy and the avenger. When I look at your heavens, the work of your fingers, the moon and the stars that you have established; what are human beings that you are mindful of them, mortals that you care for them? Yet you have made them a little lower than God, and crowned them with glory and honor.*
> *Psalm 8:1-5*

"Being unwanted, unloved, uncared for, forgotten by everybody, I think that is a much greater hunger, a much greater poverty than the person who has nothing to eat." – Blessed Mother Teresa

In this fast paced, often cold and seemingly uncaring world of today, many folks find themselves pondering the question: "Where do I fit in?" Older people are living longer, wearing out their bodies and sometimes their welcome, living beyond their resources. They look at the world with memories of a simpler, happier time when they were the ones in charge and on the rise, with their best days before them.

Today's young people are thoroughly confused by this new world with fewer opportunities, greater demands, and fewer resources. They do not really desire to depend on mom and dad. But what does one do with part-time jobs, low wages, and high costs. And when they look at their world, it is very difficult to know where they really fit in, or, if they will ever fit in at all. It is in this world with little hope that teens and young adults make some very drastic life decisions. Some choose anything that will make them feel temporarily wanted or needed. Some decide that the price of popularity is worth a few moments of feeling a part of the group. Some spend their days escaping into the world of unreality in their video games and TV shows.

Do you suppose this is the way God meant for life to be? Do you believe that God would abandon you or maybe that God never even cared about you? In the book of Job, we read about a man who did all that he thought was right, yet bad things kept happening to him. Job comes to the conclusion that God is aware of him but that God is disappointed in him and is punishing him. Job just does not know where he fits. The wonderful part of Job's story is that God is fully aware of the turmoil Job is going through, and God knows that Job is a good man. Even in the trials and tribulations of Job, God never abandons him.

This is the wonderful story we find in the celebration hymn in Psalm 8. It is a story of humankind's place in all of God's creation. The psalmist celebrates that God has placed every person in a very lofty position in the grand scheme of the creation. You and I are so valued by the Creator God that we are given dominion over all that is created. Never will we be abandoned because our Father in heaven loves us with his divine love. Each of us may be assured that we are not alone and that we do fit.

As we move through these days of Advent in anticipation of the celebration of the birth of Christ, we need only to look around us at that which was created by God to find our true meaning. No creature of our heavenly father is unwanted. Yes, some are living difficult lives. Some do exist in poverty, some without the basics of life. But no one can truly say, "I am not wanted" or "I have no place in this world." God longs to love each of us. In fact, God loves each of us so much that he offered his only Son that we might live. We are saved for eternity because of that love through Jesus Christ.

The psalmist has assured us that we have a place in this kingdom of the living God. He places each one of us firmly in the middle of God's creation with a tremendous task before us. We are charged with being God's people and caring for God's creation. Even the simplest soul can find comfort in the words found in Psalm 8, as we each realize that for all of God's creation we each have been seen as special, as important, as wanted by a loving God.

The amazing thing about this time as we anticipate the birth of Jesus is that we can be assured that our lives will always retain meaning. We fit! We are God's children! We are saved by his grace!

John Norman
New Pentecost UMC

Prayer: Loving God of creation, draw each of your children near to you during this season of anticipation. We are assured that you created us with a purpose. We are assured that no matter how low we may fall, your grace will hold us up and welcome us to your side. Let none of your children suffer without the sure knowledge that they are selected to be creatures of your kingdom and that they are blessed. Amen.

December 11

> *In the sixth month the angel Gabriel was sent by God to a town in Galilee called Nazareth, to a virgin engaged to a man whose name was Joseph, of the house of David. The virgin's name was Mary. And he came to her and said, 'Greetings, favored one! The Lord is with you.' But she was much perplexed by his words and pondered what sort of greeting this might be.*
> *Luke 1:26-29*

Life can leave us perplexed and confused at times. We make plans and envision our future only to realize our best laid plans do not always come to fruition. Just ask the high school sports star whose leg injury has left her seeking new ways of funding college. Just ask the parents of a brand new child who learned their bundle of joy will have special challenges along the way. Just ask the man recently retired who learned of his diagnosis of terminal cancer as he made plans to travel the world. In these life changing moments when the news appears bleak, we don't always feel favored and God can seem far away.

Mary of Nazareth knows about these moments. In Luke's Gospel, she is visited by the angel Gabriel. The greeting from Gabriel is simple. "Greetings favored one! The Lord is with you!" Of course, Mary is perplexed by this greeting. The greeting sounds wonderful, but what comes next is the mystery. What kind of message could a messenger of God bring me? How will this message change my life? She soon learns that she is pregnant in a most mysterious way. Most disturbing, the man she loves, the man she is engaged to marry is not the father. Mary's life is turned upside-down. She had made plans. Her life was in front of her as she married Joseph and lived a quiet life in

Nazareth raising a family in anonymity and peace. Now, the possibility existed that she could be rejected by Joseph. She could be left on her own or put to death accused of cheating on Joseph. Mary was perplexed and confused.

I personally experienced one of these moments in 2012. I received a call that my mom was taken to the hospital for dehydration. I knew she had been sick with what appeared to be the flu, but I expected her to get over it soon. In my vision of the future, my mom still had plenty of years to live life and enjoy her grandchildren. After several days of weakness in the hospital, I began to realize her condition was not improving. She continued to struggle, but the doctors and nurses were optimistic that she would eventually recover.

On July 4th, I received word my mom had taken a turn for the worse. She had gone into cardiac arrest and now was in the ICU of the hospital. Upon receiving this disturbing news, I made my way to the hospital. My mind was in shock. Receiving this kind of news was different and mysterious. I did not know what to expect when I arrived. Entering the ICU waiting room, only one person sat waiting for my arrival. The person was my mom's doctor. My mind travelled to the worst place and the news from the doctor was not much better. My mom had gone into septic shock and the prognosis was not good.

I remember sitting in the ICU waiting room that night for a long time alone. On the wall hung a little television broadcasting the fireworks on the mall in Washington D.C. I sat and pondered the happy families. I was fascinated by a little boy sitting on his dad's shoulders watching in wild eyed amazement as the burst of lights danced to the sound of patriotic music. On this night, that little boy had the world in front of him and the strength of his dad under him. He was making special memories I hope last his entire life.

That little scene brought back my own memories of my special moments with mom. I remembered the conversations. I remembered the times she encouraged me and mended a cut knee. I especially remembered her lessons of unconditional love taught simply by the way she loved her children.

In those quiet moments alone in an ICU waiting room as my world was spinning with a variety of emotions. I also realized something else. I really was not alone. God sat beside me in my grief. God's strength would continue to walk beside me the next seven days as mom hung between life and death. God's strength was with me in the moment she breathed her last and continues through the difficult road of grief. In the moments I feel the weakest, my heavenly Father lifts me on His shoulders.

Mary was perplexed by the message from Gabriel. What could it mean? Where would she go from here? One thing she knew, though, from what Gabriel told her. She would not travel this path alone. For you see, Gabriel said, "The Lord is with you." God was with Mary and God is with us as we travel those mysterious, perplexing roads called life. Regardless of what is around the curve, God's promise to be with us lets us know it's going to be OK.

David Sanders
Sunny Side UMC

Prayer: Precious Lord, thank you for your presence as we travel these mysterious roads of life. Help us to be aware of your presence on the journey. Help us to cherish the moments we have in life and realize that we can trust you regardless of what news may come our way. Amen.

December 12

The angel said to her, 'Do not be afraid, Mary, for you have found favor with God. And now you will conceive in your womb and bear a son, and you will name him Jesus. He will be great, and will be called the Son of the Most High, and the Lord God will give to him the throne of his ancestor David. He will reign over the house of Jacob forever, and of his kingdom there will be no end.'
Luke 1:30-33

Mary has a key role in the Christmas story, but she had a long personal Advent before the events in our text took place. Mary's entire life up until this point was a preparation for this moment. God did not send His angel, Gabriel, to just any young woman living in Israel. Not just any of the multitudes of unmarried girls would do to bear and raise God's son. Mary possessed some important qualities that influenced God's decision to choose her for this awesome calling.

We are told three times in this passage that Mary was a virgin. Of course God wanted purity in His Son's mother, but the fact that she was a virgin also indicated her self discipline and obedience to the Law of Moses. This also demonstrated her respect for herself and her future husband. It would seem then that God chooses to use people for His glory who are disciplined, obedient and respectful of self and others.

Another trait that we observe in Mary is humility. A good definition of humility is not thinking more or less of ourselves than God does. Mary certainly showed this in her response to Gabriel's message. "She was much perplexed" we read. This shows that she would never have considered herself worthy of a visit by an angel. It also demonstrates that she had no prior thought of her usefulness to God, but also that if He chose to send an angel to her, it must be that God considered her both worthy and useful. She accepts this as it is presented, and listens carefully to the angel's words as he prophesies to her. Humility also makes us ready to serve the Lord.

In verse 38 of this same passage Mary says to Gabriel, "Let it be with me according to your word." This indicates her willingness to be used by God for His purpose. Mary was no fool, she knew what would lie ahead for her when she was found to be pregnant. The Gossip, slander, and rejection of her community, and even divorce from her betrothed husband were all possible. Nonetheless, she trusted God and was willing to be used by Him for His purposes.

We revere Mary still today. We hold her up as an example of godliness. We give her much credit for her motherhood of, and influence on, the life of Jesus. How did she become such a famous and adored fixture of Christianity? She was self-disciplined, obedient, respectful, humble, and willing for God to use her. We can do that. With God's help we too can live our own Advent in such a way that God will use us this Christmas season to be a blessing to others in His Name.

Ed Swehla
County Line UMC

Prayer: Lord God, We thank you for this time of preparation. We ask that you influence us to live in ways that make us more and more useful to you. Fill us with your Spirit so that we may bring good news and joy to those around us. We praise you that you use simple people to carry out your plans. Amen.

December 13

Mary said to the angel, "How can this be, since I am a virgin?" The angel said to her, "The Holy Spirit will come upon you, and the power of the Most High will overshadow you; therefore the child to be born will be holy; he will be called Son of God. And now, your relative Elizabeth in her old age has also conceived a son; and this is the sixth month for her who was said to be barren. For nothing will be impossible with God." Then Mary said, "Here am I, the servant of the Lord; let it be with me according to your word." Then the angel departed from her.
Luke 1:34-38

The foretelling of the coming of Christ to Mary is a wondrous and life-altering story. Gabriel comes to a young girl around 15 years of age and tells her that she will completely change the world because she is going to deliver the Messiah. She has lots of questions about how it will happen. These are today's verses. She asks "How can this be?" and Gabriel answers those resounding words "nothing will be impossible for God." These words still her soul and she responds, "Here am I, the servant of the Lord; let it be with me according to your word." And then her story moves on and God's plan continues. Glory Hallelujah and thanks be to God.

This past February, I was blessed to go to Israel for the first time. It was a marvelous and life-changing experience. I was able to see, touch, smell, and hear the Land of the Bible. Yes, things are different than in the first century but the Spirit is still very much alive. One of the days on the trip I got to see the Church of the

Annunciation, the exact location where we believe that Mary had this very conversation with the angel Gabriel.

The church was very ornate. There where large frescos of different countries' interpretation in art of what the conversation was like between Mary and Gabriel. The towering church allowed my soul to stir and while we were there a small service was taking place. As I sat in the pew listening to the service, my mind wondered about the past, wishing I could have been there for that exceptional moment when Mary realized that she was going to carry the Christ and that it was only through the power of the Holy Spirit that this could and would happen. I was envious.

At that moment, a thought crossed my mind. I was told that I "have found favor with God." I was also around 15 or 16 years of age. It was the day that I accepted Jesus Christ as my Lord and Savior. That day I could not understand how it would happen. Being baptized, I would have Christ in my heart, but this was not my doing. Rather, I was informed that it was the work of the Holy Spirit. I was going to bring Christ into the world again. At the Church of the Annunciation, I was reminded that I am carrying the Christ.

Yes, I know the two situations are different. However, in a way we all need to remember that when a friend, a coworker, a family member, or even a complete stranger comes to know Christ as their Lord and Savior, they have just experienced a wondrous and life-altering moment just as Mary had experienced. And they begin a new life, carrying Christ within them for the world to see.

That day at The Church of the Annunciation, I understood that God's plan is continuing everyday of our lives. God is allowing the world to find His son, His love, His favor through each of us. His plan was impossible for us, though nothing is impossible for Him. Let's change the world and show everyone the Christ that is inside each of us. The first step could be just to say, "Here am I, the servant of the Lord; let it be with me according to your word."

Terry Hunter
Williamson UMC

Prayer: Gracious Father in heaven, here am I, the servant of the Lord; let it be with me according to your word and use me as I am. Allow all of us to see the impossible happen in our lives and in others today. May your Spirit overshadow each of us so that when others see us, they truly see You. In your Son Jesus's name. Amen.

December 14

> *In those days Mary set out and went with haste to a Judean town in the hill country, where she entered the house of Zechariah and greeted Elizabeth. When Elizabeth heard Mary's greeting, the child leaped in her womb. And Elizabeth was filled with the Holy Spirit and exclaimed with a loud cry, "Blessed are you among women, and blessed is the fruit of your womb."*
> *Luke 1:39-42*

Through the centuries some have wondered about Mary's rush visit to her cousin Elizabeth after the angel's visit. Gabriel appears to her alone in Nazareth one day saying, "Greetings, favored one! The Lord is with you." (Luke 1:28b) Mary is quite perplexed by this -- the angel and the greeting. But this doesn't deter Gabriel who tells Mary not to be afraid for she has found special favor with God: She will conceive in her womb and give birth to a child. His name will be Jesus, and he will be called "the son of the Most High" (vv.30-32b) – in other words, he will be the long promised and expected Messiah.

Mary grows only more perplexed by this announcement and asks how this can possibly be since she is a virgin. The angel explains that the Holy Spirit will come upon her, and so the child will be holy and called the Son of God. Then, Gabriel says, "And now your relative Elizabeth in her old age has also conceived a son; and this is the sixth month for her who was said to be barren. For nothing will be impossible with God." (vv.35-37)

I don't think there's anything surprising about Mary visiting Elizabeth. A girl who is engaged to an older man she has not yet "known" is visited by an angel who tells her she is going to become pregnant and give birth to a son who is the Messiah -- all this by the power of the Holy Spirit. Mary sounds remarkably calm and collected as she obediently responds, "Here am I, the servant of the Lord; let it be with me according to your word." (v.38) Yet, it probably took all the faith she could muster.

Given the angel's visit, the astounding news and the huge impact it will have on Mary, Joseph, the wedding plans, their families – not to mention the world – it is no accident the angel told Mary about Elizabeth. It is an invitation for Mary to get away, take in the life-changing, world transforming announcement; receive the assurance she needs and the affirmation she seeks. Mary must go and see for herself. God understands when we need a faith boost! And God provides what we need in myriad ways, large and small, subtle and obvious, if only we open our eyes, mind and heart to receiving them!

So after the angel's news Mary heads for the hills, to a small town in the hill country of Judea -- a day's walk or so. She shows up unannounced at Zachariah's place and greets her cousin Elizabeth. And it immediately starts – all the assurances and affirmations Mary needs.

Why, Elizabeth is obviously pregnant and positively radiant! And as if the sight of her weren't enough, the old gal bursts forth with a series of assurances and affirmations in just a matter of moments. As soon as Mary says hello, Elizabeth is filled with Holy Spirit and exclaims with a loud cry, "Blessed are you among women, and blessed is the fruit of your womb." (v.42) Mary isn't even showing yet. She hasn't had chance to speak a word about the angel's visit and announcement, but Elizabeth recognizes God is already at work in and through her.

Next, Elizabeth makes the very first profession of faith in the Messiah when she asks Mary, "And why has this happened to me, that the mother of my Lord comes to me?" (v.43) Elizabeth declares the baby who is just beginning to grow in Mary's womb is her Lord. Through Elizabeth's faith-full profession, Mary receives another gift of assurance and affirmation.

Another comes in both word and deed. Mary cannot see it, but Elizabeth is quick to tell Mary that she felt her own baby jump for joy the instant Mary greeted her. The baby Elizabeth is carrying will prepare the way for the Messiah, and Elizabeth's baby is already preparing the way for Mary's baby by announcing the coming Messiah with a leap of joy!

The final assurance and affirmation comes in the form of a blessing. Elizabeth blesses Mary for her faith, for believing "there would be a fulfillment of what was spoken to her by the Lord." (v.45) By faith Mary receives the news and is willing to play her part. By faith she journeys to visit Elizabeth and receives the assurances and affirmations she needs. By faith Mary is having a baby who is going to change everything – including the whole world!

Are we ready for this baby who changes everything? Including us?

Dana Overton-Garrett
Barnesville First UMC

Prayer: Gracious God, we thank you for Mary and Elizabeth who are examples of faith to us. We thank you for the assurances and affirmations you send our way to strengthen our faith when you call upon us to share in your plan of salvation that changes the world. May we be ready and help ready others for this baby who changes everything. Amen.

December 15

> *"And why has this happened to me, that the mother of my Lord comes to me? For as soon as I heard the sound of your greeting, the child in my womb leaped for joy. And blessed is she who believed that there would be a fulfillment of what was spoken to her by the Lord."*
> *Luke 1:43-45*

As soon as Elizabeth heard the sound of Mary's greeting, the child in Elizabeth's womb leaped for joy. That child in the womb was John the Baptist. From that auspicious beginning, John never slowed down, at least not until he was finally silenced by a ruthless and disturbed king.

When I became a candidate for ordained ministry, the person who was assigned to be my mentor was the late Reverend Paul Gamber. I worked as a candidate with Paul for two years and was a friend with him for several more. He was a wise, quiet and gentle man who taught me much about ministry. Yet, the one lesson I remember most was about John the Baptist.

Paul pointed out that the purpose of John's life was to point to Christ. John was a "voice crying out in the wilderness" calling on people to prepare themselves for the coming of God. Then, Rev. Gamber stated that he and I shared the same life purpose as John. Our lives are to point to Jesus.

Our scripture today gives us a glimpse of another person who took a leap to glorify God. When young Mary was visited by the angel Gabriel, her humble response was "Here I am, the servant of the Lord." No wonder her cousin Elizabeth blesses her faith. Most of us would be terrified by such a call on our lives.

This is the woman who nurtures the Son of God in the warmth of her womb, who gives birth to him in a lowly stable, who clothes, feeds and shelters him as he grows, and who holds him when his lifeless body is brought down from the cross. No wonder the church has adored this woman through the centuries. Her purpose, like that of John the Baptist, was to point to Jesus.

That is also the purpose of our lives. The implications of this simple but profound lesson are enormous. It can shake the foundations of who you are as a person. It can force you to wrestle with the idea that you are a beacon created to light the way for others. It can humble even the most powerful and influential persons.

Integrity seems to be a character trait so rare in these times; however, when we read scripture, we realize that it has been a problem from the beginning of time. John not only lived a life of integrity, but he forcefully spoke out against those who were dishonest and unjust. He challenged people to dedicate their whole lives to a righteous God. A child leaping in the womb of his mother only reveals the beginning of a life so dedicated to the good news of Jesus Christ.

We are also called to a life of relationship. As we come to realize that God is breaking forth in human history through the life of Jesus, we do not merely celebrate that birth with gifts and food and decorations. We become transformed. We cannot help ourselves. We are drawn to sharing this good news with others. We proclaim it through word, deed and song. We come to realize that we were born to glorify and share Christ with others.

Finally, Christmas has a unique way of humbling us. To borrow from Psalm 8, we ask, "What are human beings that we are thought of so highly that God would send Jesus to die for us?" In ten short days, we will be confronted by the reality of this love. Can we slow down to consider the face of that child whom God has sent?

God had a very special purpose for John the Baptist and the Virgin Mary, and God has a very special purpose for you and me. Our lives have been created to point to Jesus. We are to live lives of integrity, relationship and humility. It can all begin here, with the Advent of God in the form of a tiny baby.

Ted Keen
Ebenezer UMC

Prayer: Creator of light and life, challenge us to lead lives worthy of Christmas. Don't let this be simply a celebration. Help us to know that this season can be a transforming experience, where we can dedicate our whole lives to point to Jesus. Amen.

December 16

And Mary said, "My soul magnifies the Lord, and my spirit rejoices in God my Savior, for he has looked with favor on the lowliness of his servant. Surely, from now on all generations will call me blessed; for the Mighty One has done great things for me, and holy is his name. His mercy is for those who fear him from generation to generation.
Luke 1:46-50

At the end of the Kairos Prison Ministry weekend, we give the prisoners an opportunity to come up to the microphone and give a testimony of what God has done in their life over the last three days. Before they come up, we tell them a parable that goes something like this: "A person received a beautiful piece of furniture as a gift. It was hand made by a marvelously skilled craftsman. The recipient of the very valuable and unique gift went to the shop where the furniture was created. They proceeded to thank the saw, the drill, the hammer for their great gift."

When God transforms someone's life through our ministry, they sometimes want to thank and praise us for helping them. It is sometimes hard for them to grasp that we are only God's tool. It seems to be human nature to lift up and revere the instrument instead of the true master who skillfully uses the tool.

Mary, the mother of Jesus realized that she was only a tool in the hand of the master. She illustrates and teaches us the true nature of faith in this passage. God, through one of His messengers had spoken to Mary and revealed to her that she was the chosen one to be the mother of the Messiah. She believed the word of the Lord. Elizabeth, her cousin said, "Blessed is she who has believed that what the Lord has said to her will be accomplished"- Luke 1:45. This is the true nature of faith: **Believe God.**

Mary's response reveals three fruits of true faith:

1. Gratitude – A grateful heart is one of the true secrets to a joyful life. Whenever a person is grateful for what they have received from God their heart is filled with joy. I do not believe that it is possible to be depressed and thankful at the same moment. "My soul glorifies the Lord and my spirit rejoices in God my Savior."

2. Humility – True faith in God recognizes that all we have and all that we are is a gift from God. It is the result of God's grace. There is no place for sinful pride when true eternal life is received as a gift. Mary's heart was prepared to receive the blessings and grace of God. Here we get a glimpse into the deepest recesses of her heart. Mary was secure enough to magnify the Lord, and accept a lowly servant's attitude toward God. "The Mighty One has done great things for me."

3. Joy – True joy is what everyone is searching for. If we seek for it directly, it will always elude us. If we seek to know God and be used for His purpose, joy falls on us like rain. "My spirit rejoices in God my Savior."

Sometimes we tend to idolize and lift up others instead of seeing them as the instruments that God has used. Many years later in Jesus' ministry, a 'woman in the crowd' idolized Mary, Jesus' mother. It is recorded in Luke 11:27, "While he was saying this, a woman in the crowd raised her voice and said to him, 'Blessed is the womb that bore you and the breasts that nursed you!'" Jesus changed the focus like we try to in Kairos. (We learned it from Him) He said, "Blessed rather are those who hear the word of God and obey it!"

God wants to bless each one of us. He wants us to truly live our lives, not vicariously idolizing or envying celebrities or saints. When we hear and obey the word of God, we will truly live in relationship and fellowship with God. Jesus changes our focus away from some idealized image of others being blessed of God. He wants us to recognize and personally experience God's blessing by "hearing the Word of God and obeying it. When we do that, we will enjoy the fruits of faith just like Mary did.

Keith Harris
Christ UMC

Prayer: Dear Gracious God. Help us to trust you when you speak to us. Help us to believe what you have spoken to us. We seek the fruit of faith in so many wrong places. Help us to learn to seek you and experience the fruits of faith, hope, and love which produces joy and peace deep within our soul. Amen.

December 17

> *"His mercy is for those who fear him from generation to generation. He has shown strength with his arm; he has scattered the proud in the thoughts of their hearts. He has brought down the powerful from their thrones, and lifted up the lowly; he has filled the hungry with good things, and sent the rich away empty. He has helped his servant Israel, in remembrance of his mercy, according to the promise he made to our ancestors, to Abraham and to his descendants forever."*
> *Luke 1:50-55*

The Second World War raged in Europe during Christmas Eve 1944. It was during this time that a mother with her four young children, having abandoned their home in Ukraine with the withdrawing German army, began life anew in the harsh realities of Dieterwald, Poland. They lived as exiles from another world. The fighting was harsh and constant; air-raids and explosions, images of the wounded and dead, and the all too familiar screams of women and children being attacked throughout the night. The winter darkness was treacherous and cold.

But it was Christmas Eve! The Mother had been invited to a nearby village by two women who had prepared a Christmas celebration amidst all the confusion and chaos, and she so yearned to take the children, to provide them some joy among the pain. The mother announced to her meager family, "Tonight we're going to a party." With wonder and excitement, not aware of the danger, the children dressed for warmth by a single wick that shimmered in a saucer of oil.

The Mother and her four children, ranging from two to eight, stepped out into the snow-covered darkness, lighted only by a crescent moon, making their way to the neighboring village. Taking each by the hand of the other, they journey along the darkened way. The houses on each side of the street were scarcely noticeable, no street lights were allowed, and the windows being heavily covered seldom allowed their inadequate light to shine. Taking a short-cut across the fields, the humble family walked and walked, too excited to feel the exhaustion.

Finally they arrived! The door was already open and they stepped into what seemed like heaven itself. Lights! A whole room-full of lights! Candlelight sparkled from a small Christmas tree. Children were playing and laughing as the heavily swathed windows kept the light inside. Humble paper chains adorned the tree; delicate paper angels lifted their spirits. They sat between the women and children sitting around on the floor, and soon the room filled with singing: "Silent Night, Holy Night." Everyone caroled with delight and from memory; melodies that lifted their souls above the terror and dread of conflict and war, inspiring in them a new hope for what the future could become.

The long march back home that evening was hardly visible as the children were amazed at their pockets being filled with beautiful balls; made out of crumpled up rags, wrapped in multi-colored yarn, gathered from unravelling old sweaters. Not long afterwards the family was evacuated; icy winds of snow blew into their faces as they traveled by way of an uncovered hay wagon drawn by two bony horses. With the front still so close at hand they traveled day and night until at last it was safe to stop. They slept in drafty old barns and ate lumps of frozen bread, while on occasion drinking a cup of milk supplied by a Red Cross jeep. Though hardship and adversity was still their constant companion, the grace and mercy of God shown through by way of the warm memory of that Christmas Eve celebration, something similar to the likeness of a small candle, God's amazing love, mercy, and grace shining forth in the darkness!

Mary's song of praise, likewise sang from the midst of hardship and adversity, proclaimed through faith a renewed hope of anticipation, indeed expectation, of God's redeeming and powerful love for the world.

Advent is that time of year when the faithful should be looking with joyful anticipation, indeed jubilant expectation for the revealing of God's divine love in Jesus Christ. But too often the faithful, alongside the world, is lingering through the experiences of doubt and confusion, and therefore miss the daily breaking forth of God's mercy and grace. Mary was living in a world which was filled with oppression and persecution, a world which was cruel and harsh, but yet she is able to sing unto the Lord a song of praise and thanksgiving!

For many during the Advent season, while the celebrations and festivities bide for our time and attention, the emotions of shame and dishonor thrive just under the surface. This is the season when memories of past pain and sorrow rushes back, overwhelming and engulfing the spirit. The recollections of loss and detachment, the remembrances of damage and harm, the reflections of injury and hurt seem to outweigh the emotions of joy and delight. Therefore, it appears that the season itself causes our experiences of joyful anticipation and jubilant expectation to turn into bouts of despondency and depression, thrusting us into realms of mistrust and disbelief.

Mary would have been facing many, if not all of these very same emotions. The long-awaited and prearranged marriage to Joseph was in jeopardy, family and personal reputation was at stake, character and integrity was in question. Mary "went with haste," not away from the fray but forward into the skirmish, with conviction and faith. Mary's song proclaims that God has flipped the script of honor and shame, not in some world to come, but already in the here and now by the life and ministry of Jesus Christ.

The anticipation and expectation of the Advent season is that The Kingdom of God is breaking forth in new and powerful ways all around us, each and every moment, truly each and every day! God's mercy and grace has broken forth in Jesus Christ unto a world that delights in its power, prestige, privilege, and pride. Mary was proclaiming that the eschatological age of God was breaking forth. The Advent season announces that God's Kingdom is breaking forth. Kingdom Living declares through faith a renewed hope of joyful anticipation, definitely jubilant expectation – God's mercy, power, and grace through Jesus Christ – God's redeeming and powerful love for the world.

This Advent Season, though hardship and adversity remain constant companions in the world, may we proclaim God's breaking forth in Jesus Christ, bringing transformation and change – maybe something similar to the likeness of a small candle, God's amazing love, mercy, and grace shining forth in the darkness!

Andy Cunningham
Pomona UMC and Searcy UMC

Prayer: Most gracious and loving God, may we be mindful of the difficulties and worries which surface anew during seasons of celebration and praise. May we may lift those who struggle, praying they find healing and wholeness-- body, mind and soul. In the powerful name of Christ Jesus our Lord we pray. Amen.

December 18

Now the time came for Elizabeth to give birth, and she bore a son. Her neighbors and relatives heard that the Lord had shown his great mercy to her, and they rejoiced with her.
Luke 1:57-58

Baby time is a numinous occasion. Yes I had to look up that word the first time I saw it. Aunt Merriam and Uncle Webster told me what it meant: "supernatural, mysterious and holy; filled with the sense of the presence of the divine." At our birth we are fresh from the divine, carrying the witness of life itself. Even the most at-risk child that breathes that first breath becomes a messenger that God is with us.

As our global family grows near a record high of 7.2 billion relatives, every one of us starts as an infant. We come gasping for breath into a reality we did not choose. We are totally dependent upon other people we have never met. We have no job, no money, and no possession except the blanket snugged around us. None of us speaks the common language; we do not know the customs and laws of the land. We have no clothes, no identification and are utterly helpless. The chaos among nations and within our own nation gives evidence that many people have not developed past this first stage of life.

Even with the new laundry list of what we do not have, we see the wonderful gift that John the Baptist and mother Elizabeth have from the very beginning of life: family and friends who see this child as a gift of God's love and kindness given to a troubled world. Just like us, John did not receive things like gold, frankincense and myrrh at his birth. Only a circle of people were present and ready to celebrate the new life and God's love.

O, that every child born today could be surrounded by neighbors and family to love them. There are too many that are born into hunger, disease, war and despair that do not have this treasure of love surrounding their birth. There are too many that are born in to privilege, health, peace and comfort that do not have this treasure of love surrounding their birth.

Foster parents open their hearts and homes to surround children who need love the most. Find a foster parent in your area and give them gifts to help with their ministry of love and share in their cloud of witnesses. Get your background check and sign up to baby sit, keep the nursery, mentor at school, teach a Sunday school class, help with a pack, den, troop of children. You can be a support network for children of every status and community. Why? Because if you don't, who will? You know the powerful transformation and joy it makes for the parents, the child, yourself and God to be available to celebrate the gift each child represents.

Working with children is a treasured opportunity to see God's handwork and to experience the foundation of God's joy, grace, kindness and love. Stop reading your devotion and go celebrate a child's life and love.

John Brantley
Jackson UMC

Prayer: God, we are so busy with our Christmas plans, help us not to forget to share your Love with those who are helpless and hungry, dependent and weak. Thank you for sharing your child with us. We love you too. Amen.

December 19

> *On the eighth day they came to circumcise the child, and they were going to name him Zechariah after his father. But his mother said, "No; he is to be called John." They said to her, "None of your relatives has this name." Then they began motioning to his father to find out what name he wanted to give him. He asked for a writing tablet and wrote, "His name is John." And all of them were amazed. Immediately his mouth was opened and his tongue freed, and he began to speak, praising God.*
> *Luke 1:59-64*

"All noise is waste. So cultivate quietness in your speech, in your thoughts, in your emotions. Speak habitually low. Wait for attention and then your low words will be charged with dynamite." ~Elbert Hubbard

The noise of the Christmas season is sometimes deafening. The sounds of the mall, the excitement of the children, the blaring renditions of modern songs about the season are everywhere. And yet, we long to be drawn into the peace and hope that the season brings … a peace and hope that is shouted in the silence of the night in a stable in Bethlehem.

Early in Luke 1 we learn that Elizabeth, never having been able to conceive, is pregnant. The joy and anticipation of her husband, Zechariah, cannot be spoken or shouted but can only be reflected in his smiles and his gentle touch. God has responded to prayers asking for a miracle and Zechariah – priest, temple leader – one whose words are listened to by everyone, has questioned God's miracle. Zechariah is no longer able to speak.

Perhaps it is at this point in the story of the one we call "John the Baptist" that we learn the most about God and perhaps about ourselves. Perhaps our words and our questioning and our shouting in this busy season, keeps us from living out the beautiful time of anticipation we call Advent. We live as no example at all of the peace, calm and hope that the season tells us about. Our words are not full of the love we have for the beautiful child to be born to Mary and Joseph. The child is to be called Jesus.

Zechariah wants to follow tradition and name his first son after himself. Everyone expects it! But this is not what God desires for Zechariah to do. God wants Zechariah to name his son John, which means "God is gracious". In the silent months after he has learned of Elizabeth's pregnancy, Zechariah continues to live silently as the priest, servant, and proud papa to be what the community desires for him to be. In his silence, he has spoken louder than he ever could about his excitement for this miracle child that God has given him and Elizabeth.

There is much to be learned from this part of the Christmas story. We learn about ourselves, that perhaps our loudest testament of our love for God and for our friends and neighbors comes in our silent expressions of that love. Offering a gentle hand and soft hug to a hyper-pumped child giddy with excitement from visiting Santa Claus. Sharing Christmas goodies with a neighbor without fanfare as you spread the love of Christmas. Spending extra time in prayer for those around you, those in need, those who are hurting in some way.

It is in the silence of our lives that we speak the loudest.

And God? What do we learn about God in this story? We learn of God's ability to answer prayer with miracles. We learn that sometimes God is teaching us to be more humble at the same time that God is answering our prayer. We learn that God is fully in charge of this season of Advent as God unfolds God's story about the birth of his son. We also learn about God's response to our faithfulness.

As Zechariah quiets the crowd of friends and neighbors, he quietly says, "His name is John". God has spoken through Zechariah after all these months of silence. The message is loud and clear, God is doing something special here and Elizabeth and Zechariah are being blessed as a part of it. Zechariah's words are more powerful than they would ever be had he never been silent.

The season of Advent and Christmas is a wonderful time of excitement and joy. Perhaps it is best celebrated with moments of quiet and even silence. The real crescendo of the season comes on a quiet night, in a manger, marked by a bright star overhead. And the angels began to sing and the quiet of the night was broken. God is gracious!

John Norman
New Pentecost UMC

Prayer: Our blessed Lord God, forgive us for being too loud. We have learned to approach the time of your Son's birth with so much hustle and bustle and noise that we do not tell your story in our calm and quiet. Teach us to be your gracious servants. Still our loud voices and exchange them with quiet words of praise for our Lord, Jesus. Amen.

> *John's father Zechariah was filled with the Holy Spirit and prophesied, "Bless the Lord God of Israel because he has come to help and has delivered his people. He has raised up a mighty savior for us in his servant David's house, just as he said through the mouths of his holy prophets long ago. He has brought salvation from our enemies and from the power of all those who hate us."*
> *Luke 1:67-71*

Deliverance! Savior! Salvation! Jesus!

When I was about 12 years old, I can remember kneeling at the chancel rail and looking up at the Crucifix hanging high above the Altar. As I looked, I saw the blood stains and the face of our dying Lord Jesus. It was at that moment that I realized that Jesus, the baby born in a manger, came to earth to save me. My eyes filled with tears and I wept at the thought of this Jesus who had been my friend and brother dying a cruel death because of me. My faith in God was forever changed in that moment when I knew and that I knew Jesus Christ died for me.

Zechariah and Elizabeth were blessed by God through the power of the Holy Spirit with a child. His name was to be "John" but Zechariah couldn't speak and so he wrote the name down to share it with others. When he and Elizabeth were given this precious bundle of joy, his heart was filled with love for God. Because of Zechariah's faithfulness to God he was filled with the Holy Spirit, given his voice back and immediately began to praise God.

Zechariah's prophecy tells of the coming Savior of the world, Jesus. He speaks of God's faithfulness to God's people, you and me. How are we going to share the "Good News" of the coming Savior? Might we not also share this special time in our lives with others who don't know the Risen Lord Jesus? Invite someone today to share in the joy of the Season, the joy of a baby born in a manger, who is to be the King of Kings and Lord of Lords and frees us from the bondage of sin.

Deliverance! Savior! Salvation! Jesus!

All this is for YOU! Thanks be to God!

Liza Marler
Mt. Zion UMC

Prayer: Heavenly Father, hear the prayers of your faithful children. Help us to be like Zechariah and share the coming of our Savior, Jesus. Help us to feel your Holy Spirit and may we be led to share your love, grace and mercy to all who enter our midst. In the name of Jesus. Amen.

December 21

> *Thus he has shown the mercy promised to our ancestors, and has remembered his holy covenant, the oath that he swore to our ancestor Abraham, to grant us that we, being rescued from the hands of our enemies, might serve him without fear, in holiness and righteousness before him all our days.*
> Luke 1:72-75

Our daughter Lydia always wanted to go to Venice. When she was in second grade and asked to write about herself as an adult, she wrote, "Hometown: Venice, Italy".

When Lydia was 18, she was offered a summer internship at a business in the small town of Hampton working in their technology lab.

She was told the internship would consist of two weeks in the lab in Hampton followed by two weeks in their international headquarters in Venice! The company promised to pay for her airfare, to set her up in an apartment, to provide her with a company car, and to prepay for all of her meals in the little Italian restaurant a short walk from her apartment. This sounded like a promise too good to be true, but two weeks after she left, she returned with pictures of the pigeons in Saint Mark's Square and the gondolas on the Grand Canal.

The above scripture is part of the song Zechariah sang after the birth of his son John the Baptist. Zechariah heard one of God's promises straight from the mouth of the angel Gabriel, and he thought it was too good to be true. When told that he and his wife Elizabeth would bear a child in their old age, he said, "How can this be true? I am an old man and my wife is well along in years."

Do you ever think any of God's promises sound "too good to be true"? Zechariah was looking at the evidence before his eyes rather than trusting the word from God who sees a bigger picture. Sometimes what we see before us causes us to doubt the promises of God.

For his unbelief, Zechariah was struck mute – given plenty of time to contemplate the truth of God's promises – until the fulfillment of the promise occurred with the birth of his baby boy. When the prophecy was fulfilled, Zechariah was filled with the Holy Spirit and began to speak. What he spoke of after this long period of reflection was his certainty that "God has shown the mercy promised to our ancestors, and God does remember His holy covenant".

Zechariah became a believer that God does keep His promises, even when they seem "too good to be true".

Sherri Studdard
Aldora UMC & Ebenezer UMC

Prayer: Heavenly Father, sometimes what I see before my eyes and what I reason in my own mind leads me to believe that things are hopeless. Help me to store Your word more and more in my heart that I might know Your promises. Give me faith to believe before I can see. In Jesus' name. Amen.

> *"And you, child, will be called the prophet of the Most High; for you will go before the Lord to prepare his ways, to give knowledge of salvation to his people by the forgiveness of their sins. By the tender mercy of our God, the dawn from on high will break upon us, to give light to those who sit in darkness and in the shadow of death, to guide our feet into the way of peace." The child grew and became strong in spirit, and he was in the wilderness until the day he appeared publicly to Israel.*
> *Luke 1:76-80*

After nine months of being dumb struck, after nine long months of silence, Zechariah finally has something to say! I'm not sure if Zechariah has been bursting to talk for those long nine months. Maybe he has been reflecting the silence. Maybe he has gained deep insights after questioning the good news the angel brought him by the altar of incense in the sanctuary.

Luke testifies that the Holy Spirit fills Zechariah. Then and only then does Zechariah begin to speak. He speaks of God's abundant mercy. Think about it, there is the mercy of being noticed. God has looked, taken note, and recognized the need of God's people. God is bringing redemption. There is always mercy in redemption. God is fulfilling a promise made ages before to save God's people and is acting on that promise to do so. So there is also the mercy of a promise kept, all the more pressing because of the duration of the time of waiting. Then there is mercy in the freedom of being released from captivity of our enemies and being able to worship our God fully and without fear.

Zechariah truly has something to say. He is speaking of mercy and blessings to all of the people in the world. However, these words are not merely a statement. I believe it is more of a song, a song of mercy or even the first Christmas carol.

Yes, this could be the first Christmas song every written. The first verse of the song *"Blessed be the Lord God of Israel, for he has looked favorably on his people and redeemed them. He has raised up a mighty savior for us in the house of his servant David..."* Then we can go into the second verse of the song, which tells us more of the theology and story of redemption and the deeper into the meaning of Christmas. We can sing *"By the tender mercy of our God, the dawn from on high will break upon us, to give light to those who sit in darkness and in the shadow of death, to guide our feet into the way of peace."*

We are told of the incarnation, and it is God himself who has come to his people to set them free. The song has a foreshadowing of the cross as Zechariah sings that "he has raised up for us a mighty savior." The song proclaims our coming salvation as "the light of the world" has come to shine on "those who dwell in darkness and the shadow of death." Yes, it could be the first Christmas Carol. One would have to sing every Christmas Carol they know to equal the power and majesty of these few lines from this song of Zechariah.

Then, after singing his praise of God's tender compassion, he turns to offer his Spirit-filled song upon his son, the one who will announce God's tender mercy and give them knowledge of salvation through the forgiveness of their sins. As the Gospel continues, we know that John prepares the way of the Lord until his death

Though, it's not always that way with us. Every year we all get Christmas cards that hold out the hope and wish that we might have the joy of Christmas throughout the coming year. We put up lights around the house and on the tree. We place meaningful ornaments on the tree from past Christmas seasons. We sing Christmas carols at church and maybe just maybe in the community. And shortly after the blessed celebration of Jesus birth. After the birth of the one who can and has set us free, we pack our Christmas decorations away and gradually lose that sense of "the Christmas Spirit." We stop singing the carols and songs of Christmas, and the embers of what was a fire in our hearts gradually burn out. And Zechariah's song of mercy goes into the closet of our lives.

This time let's continue to remember that we have something to sing, so we to can prepare the way of the Lord in the hearts of all mankind until Christ comes back or until death. Praise be to God!

Terry Hunter
Williamson UMC

Prayer: Heavenly Father, fill us with your Spirit that we may turn to each other with songs of mercy, blessing, and forgiveness and live into the promises you made through Zechariah. In Jesus' name, we pray. Amen.

> *Now the birth of Jesus the Messiah took place in this way. When his mother Mary had been engaged to Joseph, but before they lived together, she was found to be with child from the Holy Spirit. Her husband Joseph, being a righteous man and unwilling to expose her to public disgrace, planned to dismiss her quietly. But just when he had resolved to do this, an angel of the Lord appeared to him in a dream and said, "Joseph, son of David, do not be afraid to take Mary as your wife, for the child conceived in her is from the Holy Spirit. She will bear a son, and you are to name him Jesus, for he will save his people from their sins."*
> *Matthew 1:18-21*

At the dawn of television broadcasting, Robert Young portrayed Jim Anderson in the idealistic family show, "Father Knows Best." Jim is a loving father in the show offering sage advice to his children. Jim was the precursor to other wise dads on TV such as Ward Cleaver, Andy Taylor, and Bill Huxtable. In these shows, the dad was portrayed as a positive role model. Someone you would want as your own father. A father a man would want to strive to become.

Somewhere along the way, this portrayal of dad in media became unfashionable. Dad needed to be portrayed realistically. The audience needed to see that dad was not perfect. In fact, he did not know best. Eventually, dad became the clown of the family. He was just an oversized child getting in as much trouble as the children.

The true reality is that dads, just like anyone else in the world, are a mixture of wisdom and folly. They struggle with the issues of life. They sometimes offer wise advice and other times do not provide the best example. Parenthood is a tough business. Children do not come with manuals and so parents do the best they can. They need positive role models to demonstrate what parental sacrifice and love is all about.

Joseph of Nazareth provides such an example in the gospel of Matthew. He learns his fiancé is pregnant. The story she tells him seems ludicrous and impossible. I imagine Joseph was hurt by this perceived betrayal and in this day and age, Joseph had options. He could send Mary away to fend for herself. He could have her stoned for adultery. But Joseph loved Mary, he would not humiliate her. His decision was to dismiss her quietly and without fanfare.

That night, an angel appears to Joseph in a dream and informs him of Mary's situation. The angel tells him to not fear to take Mary as his wife. She will have a son and this son will save the world. Upon waking, Joseph had options on how he could proceed. He could dismiss the dream as an overactive imagination. He could ignore the angel and live his life without taking care of a child that was not his own. Instead, Joseph provides the ultimate example of love and sacrifice. He chooses to marry Mary and raise Jesus as his own son.

We often hear of the dead beat dad that leaves his family so he can live as he pleases. Statistics inform us that the majority of single parent families are mom and children, but what about the dad that sacrifices? What about the dad that does the best he can to provide for his family? What about the dad that is willing to raise a child even though that child is not biologically his own? These dads are the ones we celebrate. These dads are the ones that provide the greatest examples because they demonstrate what we can become as parents. They are not perfect. They make mistakes along the way, but the desire to be the best we can is the first step toward the ideal.

Where have you gone Jim Anderson? We need you today in a world that glorifies dysfunction. We need an example of fatherhood that demonstrates the very best. We need the ideal. Oh! We know the ideal is not reality. A father or mother will never know best. Only God can provide true wisdom. But, we do need examples. We need to see how things could be. We need to strive to become what God has called us to become as parents.

We don't know much about Joseph from the Bible, but what we do know is enough. His little place and role in the Christmas story provides an example for fathers everywhere to strive for love and sacrifice. He let's us know that offering ourselves in service to God is the greatest decision we can make.

This Christmas, take the opportunity to reflect on your own family. What examples inform your expectations of parenthood? What kind of parent do you strive to be? God knows you are not perfect, but strive to be the best you can? Allow the Holy Spirit to transform you and make you into a parent of wisdom. With God working in our lives, we may just learn to know best.

David Sanders
Sunny Side UMC

Prayer: Gracious God, may your wisdom overflow our lives as we strive to become the people you created us to be. Help us to be role models for others as we demonstrate your love and sacrifice in the world around us. Amen.

> *All this took place to fulfill what had been spoken by the Lord through the prophet: "Look, the virgin shall conceive and bear a son, and they shall name him Emmanuel," which means, "God is with us." When Joseph awoke from sleep, he did as the angel of the Lord commanded him; he took her as his wife, but had no marital relations with her until she had born a son; and he named him Jesus.*
> *Matthew 1:22-25*

Dreams can be fluid and peaceful opportunities, where our bodies are preoccupied with rest, and our mind and spirit find freedom to listen, work and process what might be missed during the actions of the day. At other times, dreams are filled with confusion, fears and phobias that afford anything but rest. Then, there are divine messages that come at unexpected times.

Joseph had things planned out for his life, career and family. In one conversation he finds that in a moment his long-term plans have become obsolete. In the same conversation he finds a new purpose, a new vision and new understanding of family.

The angel reports an important message from God for which some of us pray and others dread. The night vision makes plain God's plan for Joseph: "Here is the way it's going down. Are you in or out?"

What does it feel like when someone announces plans for the family and we have no choice to change the plans? Some people withdraw, fold their cards, pick up their toys and choose not to be involved. Look how many people use drugs, food, alcohol or other things to soothe the pain and fear of this moment, rather than go with a better plan.

When the angel shows up at the foot of Joseph's bed, he clearly reminds Joe that God cares about him. He does not want Joseph to run. He wants him involved, connected and in the work.

When a loved one asks or even demands that we change a bad habit, we need to hear their love and request to be working together, instead of hearing a complaint or pushing away. Most of the time, we need God to speak through someone else for us to hear the message: "Here is the plan. I want you in. Don't back away from the challenge. I am with you."

Emmanuel! God is with us. This is the Christmas message that we begin to share. Which is the better Christmas gift: for people to be Merry or people to be with Christ. I'd pick God with me any day, especially the ones that are not so merry.

This short story feels a bit chaotic. It is like a stressful, bi-polar swing from sweet dreams to nightmare to new reality. In this one night, Joseph's world flips and spins, and yet it has been good to come through the struggle.

As you prepare for Christmas, be attentive to your dreams. Be open to God's messengers that come in both your days and nights. The message will be the same for us. God's got a plan; you are in it, and God is with us, always.

John Brantley
Jackson UMC

Prayer: God let me rest but not sleep through your call. Amen.

December 25

In those days a decree went out from Emperor Augustus that all the world should be registered. This was the first registration and was taken while Quirinius was governor of Syria. All went to their own towns to be registered. Joseph also went from the town of Nazareth in Galilee to Judea, to the city of David called Bethlehem, because he was descended from the house and family of David. He went to be registered with Mary, to whom he was engaged and who was expecting a child. While they were there, the time came for her to deliver her child. And she gave birth to her firstborn son and wrapped him in bands of cloth, and laid him in a manger, because there was no place for them in the inn. Luke 2:1-7

On January 5, 1985, my peaceful sleep was interrupted by feeling nauseated and experiencing stomach pains. After thirty minutes I realized it was not a virus but the late stages of labor. The arrival of our second child was not scheduled until January 15. As I woke my husband from a deep sleep, I knew there would be plenty of time to travel to the hospital. It took almost seventeen hours for the birth of our first child.

As we made the trip from our southwest Atlanta home, my labor pains grew intense. I encouraged Herb to drive faster, which resulted in running traffic signals. Visions of being stopped by law enforcement officers or giving birth on the side of Interstate 75 filled my brain. Even though we passed two hospitals on our hurried race, I was adamant that our child was going to be born at Crawford Hospital. Within forty-five minutes of arrival at the hospital, we welcomed our second son, who was surrounded by family and the comfort and warmth of a hospital room.

There was another woman who faced giving birth away from home and not having family nearby. For Mary and Joseph it would have been normal for them to move into a room in his parents' home until he could afford to acquire land and build a home for his wife and family. But according to Luke's Gospel they remained in Nazareth. If they made the trip back to Bethlehem, it would have taken ten days and placed a great strain on Mary. Remaining in Nazareth would have allowed Mary's family to be nearby. She settled into a familiar place awaiting the birth of her son and our Savior. She remembered that God would be with her as promised.

Unfortunately they were forced to return to Bethlehem to complete a census. As Luke tells us, Jesus was not born in the comforts of a small town surrounded by family and friends. I wonder what thoughts Mary dealt with as she and Joseph made this long trip. Would she be back at home in Nazareth when her baby was born? Would this long trip be too physically stressful? Would there be a nice room to stay in while in Bethlehem?

Joseph and Mary are in the throngs of people who have come to Bethlehem fulfilling the decree from Emperor Augustus. After completing this task, they could start their trip home and await the impending birth of Jesus. But there was just one problem stopping them. Mary went into labor. They had to quickly locate a place for the birth. Since there was a multiple of people in town for this census, no rooms were available. Imagine how frustrated this couple became as they journeyed from one establishment to another as they frantically tried to locate a place for Mary to give birth. This was not what Mary expected. Her baby was to be born in Nazareth but not in Bethlehem.

When Jesus was born, there were no doctors present, no sterile delivery room, no nurses, no family waiting the sound of a cry, no formal announcement of a town crier or a colorful layette for him to wear. Jesus entered the world to the smiles of new parents, the sound of animals in the town, and the sound of footsteps as people return to their homes. Jesus being born in Bethlehem reminds us he came to us in a midst of the chaos, of the loneliness, of the rejection, and to fulfill the promise that God made to Mary and to the world. A Savior was born to bring us peace, hope, joy and love to all.

Instead of saying Not in Bethlehem, let the words of proclamation of the birth of Jesus be the following: Yes in Bethlehem; Yes in our churches; Yes in our homes, and Yes in our communities.

Carol Scroggs
Concord UMC and Zebulon UMC

Prayer: Almighty God, we become frustrated when our expectations are not fulfilled. Help us to place our trust in you as we are guided through your presence and revelation in our lives. Amen.

December 26

> *In that region there were shepherds living in the fields, keeping watch over their flock by night. Then an angel of the Lord stood before them, and the glory of the Lord shone around them, and they were terrified. But the angel said to them, "Do not be afraid; for see—I am bringing you good news of great joy for all the people: to you is born this day in the city of David a Savior, who is the Messiah, the Lord. This will be a sign for you: you will find a child wrapped in bands of cloth and lying in a manger." And suddenly there was with the angel a multitude of the heavenly host, praising God and saying, "Glory to God in the highest heaven, and on earth peace among those whom he favors!"*
> *Luke 2:8-14*

Three times. Luke mentions where Jesus was placed after his birth three times. A manger, a manger, a manger.

It is the most recognizable symbol of Jesus' birth. Mary and Joseph are usually represented looking down at the baby lying in a simple feeding trough. This scene is echoed on Christmas cards, posters, simple drawings of children, and the sweet carol "Away in a Manger."

Our hearts are warmed by the simplicity of the manger. It reminds us of the humble beginnings of our Savior.

When we visit living nativities, it is often the animals (donkeys, goats, birds and camels) who garner the most attention. Yet, eventually, we are always drawn back to who is lying in the feeding trough. I discovered this to be true some years ago.

A small church I served in Atlanta hosted a live nativity every year. Occasionally, our church would be blessed with an actual newborn child to play the role of Jesus. Most years, however, Jesus was simply represented by one of my daughter's realistic dolls. These live nativities were always hectic. Hundreds gathered to see Mary, Joseph, several shepherds, three wise men, and numerous animals. Almost always, however, our guests (both children and adults) would walk up close to the manger to see who was lying there. Occasionally, the children (both girls and boys) would even ask to hold the doll.

Imagine that! With all the costumes we made, stable construction we completed, and exotic animals we brought in, the center of our nativity ended up being a plastic doll. Yet, that was exactly the way it should have been.

Luke mentions a child lying in a manger three times because it is important. It is the Divine Sign that a Savior has been born in the city of David. The angel gave the shepherds specifics. Not a crib. Not a blanket. Not a mother holding a child. Instead, "you will find a child wrapped in bands of cloth and lying in a manger."

Earlier, Luke mentions Augustus Caesar (Luke 2:1). I think Luke does this on purpose. The emperor is the foil for what is taking place in Bethlehem – a contrast that reveals God's true intentions for this world.

Jupiter, Venus, and their brothers and sisters were still important to the state religion. However, after Octavian had consolidated the republic, he created the Roman Empire and adopted the divine name of Augustus. Adoration and worship of Augustus as the "son of the gods" soon followed.

The Roman emperor never knew of a child born on the frontier of the empire. Within two generations, Augustus' successors had definitely heard of Jesus, because they began to systematically persecute his followers.

Eventually, these emperors would become followers of Christ, themselves. The world was never the same again.

Consider this manger again. It is the Divine Sign of the Savior. Humble shepherds are the first to hear of his birth, and they are told where to find him. God has started something truly special in history. Instead of changing the world through the powerful emperor in Rome, God chose to change the world through the birth of a poor baby in a small village on the outskirts of the empire. Now, that is a child to worship.

Ted Keen
Ebenezer UMC

> *Prayer: God, if we haven't already done so, help us to take a close look at the manger with adoration and worship in our hearts. Amen.*

December 27

> *When the angels had left them and gone into heaven, the shepherds said to one another, "Let us go now to Bethlehem and see this thing that has taken place, which the Lord has made known to us." So they went with haste and found Mary and Joseph, and the child lying in the manger. When they saw this, they made known what had been told them about this child; and all who heard it were amazed at what the shepherds told them. But Mary treasured all these words and pondered them in her heart. The shepherds returned, glorifying and praising God for all they had heard and seen, as it had been told them.*
> *Luke 2:15-20*

Have you ever though why the shepherds were the first ones to hear of the coming of the new born king? Did they catch the gaze of the Lord? Were they chosen because they worshipped and praised God as they worked day and night? The shepherds were at work that night just as they had been every night. What was so special about them that God chose them? He could have chosen to make his birth announcement to the rulers, kings or religious leaders but he chose to meet the working class in their workplace.

We don't know why the birth of our New Born King (Jesus) and the fulfillment of Old Testament prophecy was announced that night to the shepherds while they were at work.

I don't think that they had any idea that their lives were about to change forever. They worked outside under the stars and in the cold and wet of the night. Their workplace was in the fields as they protected their flocks from danger.

Were *these* shepherds chosen because they fought against the boredom of every day work? They work diligently day after day and night after night. They were men of great faith. They believed the angel who appeared to them and with confidence left their work to go to Bethlehem. To see God's promise in the flesh. After they had seen the baby Jesus just as the angel said, they told everyone about what happened. These working men were the first evangelists for Jesus.

How easy it is to lose ourselves in our work. Our Job can be all consuming. We can be tempted to not work as hard as we should because it is not challenging enough. But if we do that, we are likely to miss it when God shows up where we work.

God came to people just like you and me, not to the ones who would have questioned His announcement. God came to the ones who would believe and go.

If you ever wondered if God cared about what you do and where you work, your answer can be found in the shepherds who were at work that historic night.

Here are some questions to consider:
1. Why do you think the angel of the Lord showed up to the shepherds that night? Have you ever thought God has forgotten you in your place of work?
2. Are you catching the gaze of the Lord while you work?
3. How would your work relationships be impacted if everyone realized that God sees past your position and title?
4. We can worship God when we work diligently, pray continually and be joyful always. How can you worship God at work today?

Arianna Eberle
Culloden UMC, The Rock UMC and Yatesville UMC

Prayer: Dear Lord, Thank you for the work you have placed in my hands. Help me to see you in every place I am and in everything I do. Take this day and let it be a day I give all glory and honor to you. Please be with everyone today and keep all jealousy and pride away. In the name of the Father and the Son and the Holy Spirit.

> *After Jesus was born in Bethlehem in the territory of Judea during the rule of King Herod, magi came from the east to Jerusalem. They asked, "Where is the newborn king of the Jews? We've seen his star in the east, and we've come to honor him." When King Herod heard this, he was troubled, and everyone in Jerusalem was troubled with him. He gathered all the chief priests and the legal experts and asked them where the Christ was to be born. They said, "In Bethlehem of Judea, for this is what the prophet wrote: You, Bethlehem, land of Judah, by no means are you least among the rulers of Judah, because from you will come one who governs, who will shepherd my people Israel."*
> Matthew 2:1-6

Christmas has come! Praise be to God!

As we put away the decorations, go back to school, go back to work, and continue our lives, what has changed for us? What has happened that causes us to rethink, review and turn towards the Savior of the world?

King Herod was afraid of this little baby. Scripture tells us that everyone in his kingdom was "troubled" – I translate to "afraid". I have to wonder why? Why be "troubled", afraid? I suppose we are all afraid or troubled when change happens.

They knew that the Prophets had foretold of a shepherd, a leader who would "govern" the people of Judah. So by all rights, Herod was afraid he would lose his kingdom, and the people were afraid because they didn't know what was coming – what changes were coming. Not to mention that having "Magi" come to town to tell of this coming King.

We are preparing for a new year and change is evident, expected, guaranteed. But the one thing that will never change is the love of God, the gift of our Savior Jesus and the covering of the blood of the Lamb.

Be encouraged today by the grace of God, the coming of a Savior and the indwelling of the Holy Spirit. Let's look to this New Year with anticipation and joy in God's amazing faithfulness. "Do not fear," as Jesus said so many times.

Emmanuel – God is with us!

Liza Marler
Mt. Zion UMC

Prayer: Heavenly Father, thank you for your love and grace through our Lord, Jesus. As we embark on a New Year, help us to see the glory of your love and grace. Fill us with your Holy Spirit and help us to shine the light of Christ Jesus on others. Remind us each day of your amazing grace and guidance. In Jesus' name. Amen.

> *Then Herod secretly called for the wise men and learned from them the exact time when the star had appeared. Then he sent them to Bethlehem, saying, "Go and search diligently for the child; and when you have found him, bring me word so that I may also go and pay him homage." When they had heard the king, they set out; and there, ahead of them, went the star that they had seen at its rising, until it stopped over the place where the child was.*
> *Matthew 2:7-9*

King Herod was troubled. His kingdom was threatened. These so called wise men from the east shared news of a new king and this king was not him or in his family. In Herod's mind, there was not enough room for two kingdoms in the same land. This king child threatened his power, his prestige, his livelihood. So he devised a plan. He began to scheme. The political machinery began to spin and Herod would win at all cost. So he called the wise men to him and put his plan into action.

When I think of this conversation between Herod and the wise men, it brings to mind the villains in the Saturday morning cartoons. I see him rubbing his hands as he speaks in an ominous voice persuading the wise men to do his bidding. "Go to Bethlehem, search for the child, and let me know when you find him." Of course, Herod's intentions are pure. He only wants to pay homage to this new king born in his kingdom. No way would he harm a child. Right?

King Herod represents the pattern of politics in a broken world. Win at all cost. The ends justify the means. The other side is wrong. I am right so I will do whatever it takes to get my way. This mindset creates an "us versus them mentality" with the enemy needing to be defeated and destroyed. To be fair to Herod, he didn't invent this mentality. People have a tendency to hold on tight to their perceived kingdoms. Any time our power, our prestige, our livelihood is threatened, the first reaction is to act with hostility. We need to neutralize the threat. Many wars are fought for this reason. We don't have enough room for another kingdom in our world.

This passage is a collision of kingdoms, but not the kind of kingdom represented by Herod. While Herod was born in a palace, Jesus was born in a simple barn and laid in a feeding trough. While Herod was king of a geographical region, Jesus came to rule the hearts of humanity. While Herod wanted power for himself, Jesus came to lay his life down as a sacrifice for the world.

The difference between Herod's kingdom and Jesus' Kingdom is where each places their focus. Herod saw his kingdom as his right. The people served him and nothing or no one would threaten that power. He lived in luxury while the people suffered. He hung out with the well to do and the movers and shakers of the world. Jesus, on the other hand, came among the people. He came to serve. He came to bring new life. He hung out with sinners and the despised of society.

Jesus' kingdom can be strange and different. It's not like the political worlds we so often encounter where division and hatred is the order of the day. Jesus' kingdom collides with the world's kingdoms offering unity and peace. His kingdom comes offering wholeness and healing. His kingdom is not of this world.

Of course, this collision of kingdoms is not just present in the geopolitical world of politics. This collision also comes to our personal lives as well. We may not rule over great kingdoms. We may not have many people under our charge, but we do form kingdoms when our way becomes the only way. We form kingdoms when our selfish desires, our perceived power and prestige orders the way we view the world. A kingdom is formed when we shut out the opinions and perspectives of others as a threat.

Into these personal kingdoms, the Kingdom of God collides, threatening our security with what we may have to surrender. We may have to abdicate the throne. We may have to allow another king to take our place and reorder our world. We may need to view the world around us with different eyes.

The overarching truth is that when God's kingdom collides with our own, we have a choice in how we will respond. We can be troubled like Herod. We can rid ourselves of this threatening King Jesus who comes to change our world. We can decide that there is not enough room for two kings.

Another option is to be like the wise men. They didn't call them wise for nothing. They weren't threatened by another kingdom; they were willing to leave their own kingdoms and find this new king that came to change the world. They didn't send envoys or people ahead of themselves looking for a king. They followed a star and didn't quit. They persevered until they came to a simple peasant house where Jesus lived. These wise men teach us that when God's kingdom collides into our own, maybe it's time to surrender the keys. Maybe it's time to realize that only God's kingdom is eternal. Herod's kingdom and our own will fade away, but the Kingdom of God is forever.

David Sanders
Sunny Side UMC

Prayer: Thank you Jesus for bringing your kingdom to rule our lives. May we bow down before you and give praise to the King of kings and Lord of lords. Amen.

December 30

> *When they saw that the star had stopped, they were overwhelmed with joy. On entering the house, they saw the child with Mary his mother; and they knelt down and paid him homage. Then, opening their treasure chests, they offered him gifts of gold, frankincense, and myrrh. And having been warned in a dream not to return to Herod, they left for their own country by another road.* Matthew 2:10-12.

The light in the foreground was bright in the midst of the blackest of nights. What was it? My wife in the front passenger seat looked all around for the moon and could not find it. Was this the moon? We decided it was simply too small to be the moon. No moon in the dark sky must have meant it was a new moon tonight. Yet, the small, bright light remained. It seemed to beckon us down the road. Eventually, we stopped paying attention to the light and it disappeared. We never discovered what it was.

I am so glad the wise men paid attention. Whatever they saw was a mystery, but it inspired them to take a journey. They had read the prophecies, studied the astronomy, and gathered gifts appropriate for a king; yet, they still had no idea. Nevertheless, they paid attention and took the journey.

We love the story of the visit of the Magi. We tell it every Christmas and sing about it in our churches. Pictures of the wise men adorn our Christmas cards. There is something fascinating about exotic, foreign wise men visiting our Savior in Bethlehem that captures our imaginations.

Nevertheless, Matthew the gospel writer is working on a longer story that is not simply sweet and lovely. What he begins to tell us here is shocking. Jesus is the true king!

This is a shocking truth, not simply because of Jesus' humble birth. It is most shocking because there are others – ruthless others – who claim to be the true king. Most notable among these is Herod, and he poses a real threat to Jesus. The threat is so real that Joseph takes his new family with him and flees to Egypt.

We soon discover that Herod dies. Three of his sons divide up his kingdom, and one of those sons, Herod Antipas, will play a significant and dangerous role in the unfolding story of Jesus.

However, before we get ahead of ourselves, we need to remember the wise men from the East, who came to bow before a child long before others would call him "King of the Jews." They came bearing gifts.

Gold. The precious metal. Synonymous with wealth and power. A gift fit for a king.

Frankincense. The prized incense. Used in the Tent of Meeting while holy sacrifices are offered to the Lord.

Myrrh. The sweet perfume. Nicodemus would use aloe and myrrh to anoint the lifeless body of Jesus.

Strange to us today, these were thoughtful and symbolic gifts for the baby Jesus. Later in the story, Matthew will tell us of another wealthy and supposedly wise man who gives gifts to Jesus. Those gifts are by no means thoughtful. They are horrific.

Pilate's soldiers will adorn Jesus with a purple robe to mock him. They will place upon the King of Kings a crown of thorns. The throne Pilate gives to Jesus is a cross of unbearable agony.

Matthew tells a story that begins beneath a beautiful, bright star and leads to ungodly, sobering darkness (Matthew 27:45). Did the wise men know? Were their gifts meant to symbolize the death of the king to whom they were paying homage? We do not know.

What we do know is that the story doesn't end with a death on a cross. What we do know is that God brought a life and light into the world through Mary. What we do know is that Jesus brings eternal life and light to the world. What we do know is that we never have to live in darkness again.

Years ago, wise men from the East paid attention to a bright light, took a journey of faith, and sought answers. We should do likewise.

Ted Keen
Ebenezer UMC

Prayer: Almighty God, as a new year is about to dawn, let us not forget this Christmas season. Let it shine bright in our lives, as we seek to be the disciples you have called us to be. Amen.

December 31

> *In the beginning was the Word, and the Word was with God, and the Word was God. He was in the beginning with God. All things came into being through him, and without him not one thing came into being. What has come into being in him was life, and the life was the light of all people. The light shines in the darkness, and the darkness did not overcome it... And the Word became flesh and lived among us, and we have seen his glory, the glory as of a father's only son, full of grace and truth.*
> *John 1:1-5,14*

John's Gospel confirms for us that Jesus is not an afterthought. The Word is present at creation. The Word is one part of the reality that is God. The 'image' of God in us is that same Word.

It is fascinating to think about the systems of characters, marks, cuts, etchings and symbols that have been developed to become the most sophisticated collection of communication in the world.

I write this devotion in preparation of traveling to Moscow on a mission trip for the North Georgia Conference, as we begin a ten-year covenant with the churches in the Moscow area. I have been studying some basic travel words and phrases without much success. The sounds are so different from my experience. Even the Russian alphabet is so different. Sounding out our symbols sometimes makes it even more difficult.

The central focus of this trip is to cross some of the barriers and build bridges by traveling there and moving in for a time. We will follow up over the next ten years, exchanging groups and teams who will move in with each other and learn from being with one another in Christ.

To save all the expense, we would could Skype or Facetime. It would be less expensive to make a phone call, email or snail mail letters and photos. Yet, there is something important, powerful and meaningful about being present with other people. Imagine what it would be like for all the people who meet their spouse on the internet, if they tried to keep the relationship going and never actually met for the duration of their vows, "until we are parted by death." There would be one key element missing: The part about the being in the meat, the flesh, the present reality.

God speaks the Word and creative action begins and unfolds. The stages and processes of formation, development and order are proven in the flesh. God is not just an idea or concept of the mind. God speaks the Word and God's good things come into being.

One of the mystery questions that kids and philosophy students debate is the ole' "If a tree falls in the woods, and there is no one there to hear it, does it make a noise." I have a definitive answer to that one. If indeed God made the tree and it falls in the woods and no one else is there to hear, it still thunders and crashes down with cracking and rumbling and a thud. Why do I know? God is always there to hear. We are never totally alone.

From the empty order-less void, God speaks the Word and life and relationship come crashing and exploding.

In preparation for Christmas, one of our family traditions is to have a "once-live-now-cut" Christmas tree with decorations and little white lights and an angel sitting on the top. Every year for the last 12 years, at some point between the middle of December to the middle of January, our tree comes crashing to the ground in the middle of the night.

We have tried a variety of stands, strings and other remedies, but it is almost a tradition that we expect. We may or may not lose some precious decorations that way; the tree may never stand straight before or after the fall. The one thing I can count on is God speaking to me when it does fall.

God reminds me of this: "Because you are fallen, Christ has taken the fall for you." I don't think it's a good idea going around knocking over people's trees on purpose, but it might get their attention and remind them it is not about the presents underneath the tree. It is that Christ's tree has been lifted up for us.

This past year we went LED. Most of the old strands had missing lights and unsafe, taped repairs. New lights were in order. I like the idea of the new lights. They last four times as long, they use eighty percent less electricity, and they are now affordable. There is a catch to the strands we bought. There are incredible BRIGHT! You may have seen those new high-beam headlights that are blue-hot-white that blind you even on the low beams. I have 250 of their little cousins on our tree.

We used to like to sit around the tree and sing, pray and take some family time on as many nights as we didn't have dinners or parties. But the lights were so bright it was a bit unpleasant to stare at them. I didn't actually notice it was a problem until I was standing in my neighbor's kitchen, and they commented on how bright our Christmas tree was this year. It's no longer a silent night at our house; they scream out into the darkness.

But light in dark places and dark times is good. The Word spoken in our hearts and homes is the life we need for the chaos around us. We need the glory, power and presence with God in our households. The creative, life giving Word and the bright Light that eradicates darkness are the gifts we need in order to be full of Grace and Truth.

The truth about Christmas is that we fill our stockings and stomachs with treasure and treats, when we need to be filled with Grace. Grace is God's expression of love that explains why God speaks the Word with us, Light's our path and trusts us with Truth. It continues to be the season of Christmas and the world needs gifts of Word, Light and Grace. Will you give them? They are already paid for and need a heart to call home.

John Brantley
Jackson UMC

Prayer: God continue to speak your Word in my life; let your light shine through me; trust me to share your Grace and Love. Amen.

Contributors

Rev. John Brantley wrote devotions for December 2nd, 18th, 24th, and 31st. He is also co-editor of this book. John is the pastor of Jackson UMC in Jackson, Georgia.

Rev. Andy Cunningham wrote the devotion for December 17th. He is the pastor of Pomona UMC and Searcy Memorial UMC, both in Griffin, Georgia.

Rev. Arianna Eberle wrote the devotion for December 27th. She is the pastor of three churches: The Rock UMC in The Rock, Georgia; Yatesville UMC in Yatesville, Georgia; and Culloden UMC in Culloden, Georgia.

Rev. Keith Harris wrote the devotions for December 6th and 16th. He is the pastor of Christ UMC in Forsyth, Georgia.

Rev. Terry Hunter wrote the devotions for December 5th, 13th, and 22nd. He is the pastor of Williamson UMC in Williamson, Georgia.

Rev. Ted Keen wrote the devotions for December 7th, 15th, 26th, and 30th. He is the pastor of Ebenezer UMC in Forsyth, Georgia.

Rev. Liza Marler wrote the devotions for December 8th, 20th, and 28th. She is the pastor of Mt. Zion UMC in Smarr, Georgia.

Rev. John Norman wrote the devotions for December 10th and 19th. He is the pastor of New Pentecost UMC in Winder, Georgia.

Rev. Dana Overton-Garrett wrote devotions for December 3rd and 14th. She is the pastor of Barnesville First UMC in Barnesville, Georgia.

Rev. David Sanders wrote the devotions for December 11th, 23rd, and 29th. He is the pastor of Sunny Side UMC in Sunny Side, Georgia.

Rev. Carol Scroggs wrote the devotion for December 25th. She is the pastor of Concord UMC in Concord, Georgia and Zebulon UMC in Zebulon, Georgia.

Rev. Ken Stephens wrote the devotion for December 9th. He is the pastor of Forsyth UMC in Forsyth, Georgia.

Rev. Sherri Studdard wrote the devotions for December 4th and 21st. She is the pastor of Aldora UMC and Ebenezer UMC, both in Barnesville, Georgia.

Rev. Ed Swehla wrote devotions for December 1st and 12th. He is the pastor of County Line UMC in Griffin, Georgia.

Rev. Richard Winn wrote the introduction to this book. He is the District Superintendent of the Griffin District in the North Georgia Conference of the United Methodist Church.